W9-AFB-658

4-7

COCTEAU
ON THE FILM

Orphée: Heurtebise and the Princess are condemned for infringing the rules of their office. (Courtesy National Film Archive of the British Film Institute)

COCTEAU
ON THE FILM

Conversations with
JEAN COCTEAU

recorded by
ANDRÉ FRAIGNEAU

Translated by
Vera Traill

WITH A NEW INTRODUCTION BY
GEORGE AMBERG

DOVER PUBLICATIONS, INC.

NEW YORK

Southern Seminary Library

18798

PN 1998.A3 C7613
111796

Copyright © 1972 by Dover Publications, Inc.
All rights reserved under Pan American and
International Copyright Conventions.

This Dover edition, first published in 1972, is an
unabridged republication, with corrections, of the
English translation originally published by Dennis
Dobson Ltd., London, in 1954 as part of their
series "International Theatre and Cinema" (Herbert
Marshall, general editor). The present edition is
published by special arrangement with Dobson
Books, Ltd.

The original French edition, titled *Jean Cocteau:
Entretiens autour du cinématographe / recueillis
par André Fraigneau,* was published by Éditions
André Bonne, Paris, in 1951 as part of their series
"Encyclopédie du Cinéma" (André Fraigneau, gen-
eral editor).

A new Introduction has been written specially
for the present edition by George Amberg, and
additional illustrations have been included.

International Standard Book Number: 0-486-22777-4
Library of Congress Catalog Card Number: 79-136299

Manufactured in the United States of America
Dover Publications, Inc.
180 Varick Street
New York, N. Y. 10014

INTRODUCTION
TO THE DOVER EDITION

THE lively conversations recorded here consist of questions and answers about and around the cinema: pertinent questions prepared by a knowledgeable interviewer and unpredictable answers by Cocteau. Yet his answers, although informal and often rambling, are not as spontaneously improvised as they may appear. For even when he digresses, they refer to familiar themes recurring in his extensive published work, and they are therefore ultimately illuminating. The most significant of those pervasive themes is his preoccupation, if not his obsession, with the predicament of the poet in a hostile and uncomprehending world. In Cocteau's definition, poetry must be understood as a generic term. A poet, then, is not only an author who writes poetry: a poet is a creator endowed with a particular vision and sensibility that magically transform the world of experience into works of art of many kinds. Cocteau's biography, as it emerges from his writings, tells the story of a haunted existence in which the private person, the public image and the artistic accomplishment are inextricably interwoven. He speaks of himself as "the lie that tells the truth." There is no sharp division between truth and fiction, between his life as actually lived and its manifestations in poems, novels, plays, essays, paintings, films or any of the many other activities he pursued. To those perplexed by this prodigious versatility, he once said, "I have been accused of jumping from branch to branch. Well, I have—but always in the same tree."

Therefore, by his own insistence, Cocteau's films must be appreciated in the context of his whole creative work, and therefore, too, his comments on the cinema are at the same time fragments of an autobiography as well as of his general views about art and artists, the public and the critic. He suggests that "a film, whatever it might be, is always its director's portrait." Without in the least underestimating the significance of his productions, he insists, "Film-making isn't my profession. Nothing compels me to direct film after film." Even when speaking about the cinema as art, he specifies that "for me, [it] is only one medium of expression among others." A medium, though, that is preeminently visual. Cocteau is precise on this point: "for me the image-making machine has been a means of saying things in visual terms instead of saying them with ink on paper," the implication being that writing and movie-making are dealing essentially with the same things. In his own estimation, he is a man of letters first and foremost who also makes films. On the other hand, there is more than a shade of vanity or pose in the casualness he assumes when talking about his cinematic proficiency, as though anxious to preserve his amateur status while yet accepting the praise. Throughout the interviews he avoids consistently the terminology of the professional film-maker, while freely revealing many production secrets of his own discovery or invention. It seems that he is, with ample justification, proud of his technical mastery precisely because the cinema is not his primary metier.

While Cocteau has endlessly theorized and speculated about the art and craft of the various literary genres, his approach to the art and craft of the cinema was largely pragmatic. In 1930, when he made his first film, *The Blood of a Poet*, he enjoyed a firmly established reputation in the realm of letters but he admits, "I didn't know anything about film art. I invented it for myself as I went along . . . ." In spite of his lack of experience, this first venture turned out to be a film of genuine merit and lasting fame. Subsequently he wrote and directed several other undisputed masterpieces, a record of excellence that conveys authority to his pronouncements. Although based on cumulative experience and supported by tangible evidence, they are mostly observations after the fact. They do not presume to formulate or advocate a coherent theory of film. Indeed, the dissimilarity of his productions, each one distinct and unique in style and character, virtually precludes the notion of an all-embracing theory. In the interviews, the absence of references to other films, as well as other film directors, indicates a notable lack of interest in the cinema in general. Only once, in answer to a pointed question, he asserts summarily that "the best films have been made by the Russians." However, in spite of his admiration for the montage principles promoted by Eisenstein, Cocteau attempts no close analysis, and he was totally unaffected by either the theories or the techniques of the Soviet directors. In his apodictic statement that "montage is style," he uses the term conventionally as a synonym for editing.

What makes Cocteau's concept of the cinema virtually unique is his persuasion that the cinema is ideally a poetic medium, different from verbal poetry but equally valid, flexible and expressive, an art of concrete visual images instead of symbolic or metaphorical ones. He submits that "there is nothing we cannot convey in a film, provided we succeed in investing it with a force of expression sufficient for changing our phantasms into undeniable facts." It is especially the concreteness of the screen events that fascinates him "because they occur in front of the eyes." The film appears as a means to make plastic poetry by transforming thoughts into images of greater immediacy and potency than verbal ones. If film is action by definition, it is poetry in action by implication. A major problem, though, of which Cocteau became increasingly aware apparently resided not in any inherent limitations of the medium but in the limitations of the public's comprehension. Rightly or wrongly, he complains that the audience is capable of recognizing poetry only if it appears in conventional guise, to wit, in the metered form and high-flowing language to which it is accustomed. "The public believes, if the language is not poetic, that it is not a film of poetry. Whereas a poet should not be concerned with poetry; the poetry must pour forth by itself. The text must be very dry and simple. The poetry must emerge out of the organization of images." In a similar vein, he says, "the public prefers poetic poetry, fantastic fairy plays, and rebels against anything that requires a personal effort of fantasy and magic." Finally, in the conversations, he arrives at the conclusion that "mystery exists only in precise things."

Although not an altogether original discovery, especially with the surrealists noisily active all around him, it had not been stated so unequivocally before. Moreover, as the director pointed out himself, it is a clue to an understanding of his "poetic" films: according to his credo, they should be anti-lyrical, anti-symbolical, anti-psychoanalytical and, most of all, anti-metaphysical. He quotes several instances in which he demonstrates how this principle works in cinematic practice. Significantly, Cocteau called the enigmatic events in *Blood of a Poet* "documentary scenes from another realm." The background for this quaint description was his consistent endeavor to dissociate himself from the surrealist movement, with which he was engaged in a running feud. However, his protestations notwithstanding, several of his films are rich in surrealistic imagery, and the more fascinating for it. The question of primacy, then so important to him, has since lost its significance. It hardly harms his reputation as an original creator to recognize that he responded intuitively to the surrounding climate of aesthetic sensibility in which surrealism prevailed.

As a poet of language, Cocteau was forever

mindful that "poetry imitates a reality of which our world has but an intuition"; as a poet of the cinema, he believed that "the more one touches the mysterious, the more it is necessary to be realistic." Judging by such films as *Orpheus*, this must be read as a practical working rule rather than the proposal of a new aesthetic. Presumably the operative factor in this experience of the real is the evidence of the eye, which Cocteau assumes to be objective and incontrovertible. Hence the broad generalization that "all films are realistic in that they *show* things instead of suggesting them in words. What is seen is seen." Taken on its face value, this is a rather questionable statement as it does not specify what precisely is seen or how it is perceived or in which way it affects the viewer. But then, overstatements, inconsistencies and "illogicalities," a word coined by Cocteau, abound in the conversations, as indeed elsewhere in his work. He admits candidly that "contradictions are the fabric we're made of." On reading the conversations, it becomes obvious how futile it would be to attempt a summation of Cocteau's theoretical persuasions. His statements cohere by virtue of his vital personality rather than on the basis of a definable rationale, and they are validated by his creative accomplishments. It seems fitting to end with a vision appended to a printed edition of *Blood of a Poet*: "With the cinema, death is killed, literature is killed, poetry is made to live a direct life. Imagine what the cinema of poets might be."

GEORGE AMBERG

LIST OF ILLUSTRATIONS

COCTEAU
ON THE FILM

Le Sang d'un Poète: the artist-poet (Enrique Rivero) and the statue (Lee Miller). (Courtesy Herman G. Weinberg)

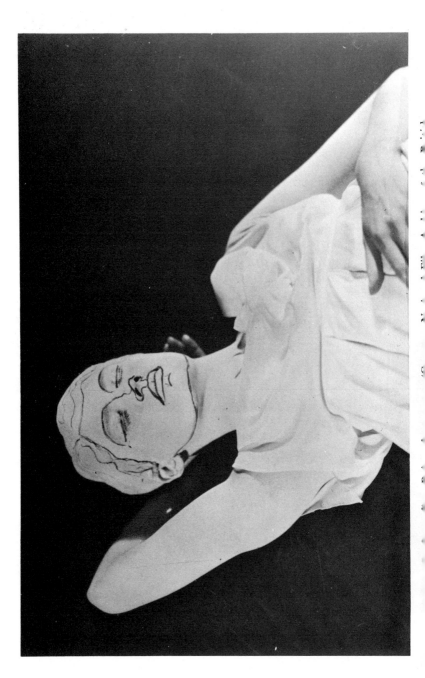

Le Sang d'un Poète: one of the visions in the hotel. (Courtesy Herman G. Weinberg)

Le Sang d'un Poète: the statue reveals herself. (Courtesy Herman G. Weinberg)

Le Sang d'un Poète: the suicide of the artist-poet.   (Courtesy Herman G. Weinberg)

JEAN Cocteau occupies a unique place in the cinematograph of our day. He was the first among the major poets to become interested in films as a medium of artistic expression. He learned the technique of film-making, or, more exactly, he re-invented it for his own personal use. Thus he created *cinematic poetry*, an exciting addition to the poetry of the theatre and of the novel, of graphic art and choreography, with which he had previously enriched French Art.

Knowing his gifts in the domain of the 'poetry of criticism', I ventured to hope that Jean Cocteau would one day give us a book about the cinema which would be for the problems of film art what *Secret Professionnel* was for literature: a collection of thoughts and recipes, reminiscences and opinions, a document all the more valuable as it would be written by an artist who was not formed in cinematography but had come to it from the other Arts.

Jean Cocteau (who had barely recovered from a surgical operation which had prevented his going to New York to present his film, *Orphée*) agreed to my suggestion—but only on condition that he would not write the book but speak it to me. He said that he preferred the warmth and spontaneity of a friendly talk to the writer's solitude. This is how the form of this book was decided upon, and our unscripted conversation, taken down in shorthand during a stay in the country where nothing came to distract us, has preserved (as Jean Cocteau wished) the freedom and the freshness of improvisation.

I had intended my questionnaire to bear exclusively on 'things cinematic', but as Jean Cocteau's lively mind rebels against any limitations, our talk, or, rather, his answers, although they did not leave out any of the precise details and fascinating secrets of the trade that I had hoped to hear, kept making sorties into wider areas. As a result, our dialogue is full of sidelights into various problems: Art in general, the psychology of the audience, and of the critics, style, and duration. It is the pathetic confession of a creator in the clutches of his dæmon.

At one stage of our dialogue (in which I was conscious of playing somewhat feebly the role of Eckermann to Cocteau's Goethe) he declared that 'every great artist, even if he is painting a window shutter or a peony, is always drawing his own portrait'. Our conversation on The Film bears this out. It draws an unpremeditated and faithful portrait of a Poet (in the sense that word had in antiquity—the maker), that is to say, of a man who places all the resources of his genius and of his hands at the service of the Spirit.

A.F.

A.F. I'd like this dialogue of ours to bear exclusively upon your activity in films, my dear Jean Cocteau. Would you be willing to approach our conversation from that angle?

J.C. I can't do that, because for me the cinematograph is only one medium of expression among others. Speaking about it will inevitably lead me into other paths. I use the word *cinematograph* deliberately, in order to avoid any confusion between the medium it expresses and that which is commonly called the *cinema*, a somewhat dubious Muse in that it is incapable of waiting, whilst all the other Muses wait, and should be painted and sculpted in waiting poses.

Whenever people see a film for the first time, they complain about some passages being too long or too slow. But quite apart from the fact that this is often due to the weakness of their own perception and to their missing the deep underlying design of the work, they forget that the classics, too, are full of passages that are long-winded and slow, but are accepted because they are classics. The classics must have faced the same reproaches in their lifetime. The tragedy of the cinematograph lies in its having to be successful immediately. It takes such a vast sum of money to make a film that it is necessary to get that money back as soon as possible by massive takings. That is a terrible, almost insurmountable handicap. I have just said that Muses should be represented in attitudes of waiting. All Arts can and must wait. They often have to wait for the death of their makers before they are able to live. Can, then, the cinematograph rank as a Muse? Besides, Muses are poor. Their money is invested. But the cinema Muse is too rich, too easy to ruin at one go.

To this we must add that, for the public, films are just a pastime, a form of entertainment which they have been accustomed, alas, to view out of the corners of their eyes. Whereas for me the image-making machine has been a means of saying certain things in visual terms instead of saying them with ink on paper.

A.F. Can you give me a more explicit definition of the *cinema* as a form of mass entertainment, and also tell me what you understand, in contrast, by the *cinematograph* as a medium of self-expression? I think that this would help readers to grasp the distinction you so persistently draw between the two terms.

J.C. What is commonly called 'cinema' has not been, up till now, a pretext for thought. People walk in, look (a little), listen (a little), walk out, and forget. Whereas the cinematograph, as I understand it, is a powerful weapon for the projection of thought, even into a crowd unwilling to accept it. *Orphée*, for instance, irritates, intrigues and shocks, but forces people to discussions with others and with their own selves. A book has to be read and re-read before it comes to occupy its rightful place. And cinema managers have noticed that some spectators of *Orphée* returned to see it several times and brought other spectators with them. Besides, however inert and hostile an audience may be, it enables a few attentive individuals to see the film. Without such audiences, my message couldn't have reached the few unknown spectators for whom it was destined. You might say that if a film falls flat the message dies. Of course. And with *Orphée* I took enormous risks. But I was convinced that in the case of an unusual and difficult film, the curiosity that brings people to see it is stronger than the laziness that keeps them away. Every day I receive letters which show that I was right.

Their authors usually complain about the audience with which they found themselves locked in for the duration of the performance. But they forget that it's that very audience that enabled them to see the film at all.

A.F. I was struck by an expression you used earlier on: 'the image-making machine'. Do you mean that you use cinematic images just as a writer uses literary images?

J.C. No. The cinematograph requires a syntax. This syntax is obtained through the connection and the clash between images. No wonder that the peculiarity of such a syntax (our style) expressed in visual terms seems disconcerting to spectators accustomed to slapdash translations and to the articles in their morning paper. If the wonderful language of Montaigne were transposed into images, it would be as difficult for such spectators to watch as it is difficult for them to read his writings.

My primary concern in a film is to prevent the images from flowing, to oppose them to each other, to anchor them and join them without destroying their relief. But it is precisely that deplorable flow that is called 'cinema' by the critics, who mistake it for style. It is commonly said that such and such a film is perhaps good, but that it is 'not cinema', or that a film lacks beauty but is 'cinema', and so on. This is forcing the cinematograph to be mere entertainment instead of a vehicle for thought. And this is what leads our judges to condemn in two hours and fifty lines a film epitomizing twenty years of work and experience.

A.F. Now I understand how much it meant for you, at a given moment in your career, to discover the cinematograph as a vehicle for thought—thought which you had previously expressed in so many different ways. But did you find a greater freedom in that new medium?

J.C. No. Even if one is free to do as one pleases, there are, alas, too many heavy burdens (capital, censorship, responsibility towards the actors who agree to being paid later) to be what I would call completely free.

I am not thinking of actual concessions, but of a sense of responsibility which directs and restricts us without our even being fully aware of it. I've been completely free only with *Le Sang d'un Poète* because it was privately commissioned (by the Vicomte de Noailles, just as Bunuel's *L'Age d'or*), and because I didn't know anything about film art. I invented it for myself as I went along, and used it like a draughtsman dipping his finger for the first time in Indian ink and smudging a sheet of paper with it. Originally Charles de Noailles commissioned me to make an animated cartoon, but I soon realized that a cartoon would require a technique and a team non-existent at that time in France. Therefore I suggested making a film as free as a cartoon, by choosing faces and locations that would correspond to the freedom of a designer who invents his own works. Moreover, I've often been helped by chance (or at least by what is commonly called chance but never is for one who lets himself be hypnotized by a task), including even the petty vexations of the studio, where everybody thought I was mad. Once, for example, as I was nearly at the end of *Le Sang d'un Poète*, the sweepers were told to clear up the studio just as we had started on our last shots. But as I was about to protest, my cameraman (Périnal) asked me to do nothing of the kind: he had just realized what beautiful images he would be able to take through the dust raised by the sweepers in the light of the arc lamps.

Another example: as I didn't know any film technicians, I sent out postcards to all the cameramen in Paris, giving them an appointment for the next morning. I decided to take the one who would come first. It happened to be Périnal, thanks to whom many images of *Le Sang d'un Poète* can vie with the loveliest shots of our time. Unfortunately, in those days a silver salt was used in film printing, which was done at a pace impossible today. This is why cinematic Art is so fragile. A very old copy of *Le Sang d'un Poète* is as bright and shows as much contrast as any modern American film, whereas more recent copies look like old copies and weaken the whole effect of the film.

Although this too is arguable. To quote an instance: a friend of mine, whose intelligence I respect, detested *La Belle et la Bête*. One day I met him at the corner of the Champs-Elysées and Rue La Boëtie. He asked me where I was going and whether he could come with me. I said, 'I'm going to work on the subtitling of *La Belle et la Bête*, and I'd hate to subject you to such an ordeal'. He came along nevertheless, and I forgot him in a corner of the little cinema. I was working with my chief editor on a very old strip, almost unpresentable, grey and black and covered with stains and scratches. At the end of the projection I went back to my friend, and he announced that he found the film admirable. I concluded that he had seen it in a new perspective, rather as we do in film societies when we are shown old films in a disastrous condition, since they are the only copies left.

A.F. It seems to me that such strokes of chance, and all the miseries and splendours of film making, coupled with the difficulty of understanding a film, that is, to see and hear it with sufficient attention in the course of one fleeting projection, make it difficult, if not altogether impossible, for a message expressed in a film to have any *lasting* existence.

J.C. Yes, indeed. The inevitable *invisibility* of any work of art which doesn't conform to public habits which make things visible—I mean, an invisibility arising from habits which were themselves acquired through contact with things that were not visible originally, but which have become visible through habit—this invisibility is an almost insuperable problem for those who treat the cinematograph as an Art, as a vehicle of thought. It is almost impossible to solve it without resorting to some subterfuge which would make that thought visible in the immediate present, but would condemn it for the future. There is no future for a film. Or, at best (provided the American laws become more sensible and one ceases destroying a story told in one manner for the sake of being able to retell it in another) the film will have a future of a sort with film clubs and a handful of amateurs. A film thus takes a reverse course compared to that followed by other works of art, which start on a small scale and reach a big one later, when they have proved their worth. The industrial machine forces films to begin on a large scale; after which they may live to reach a small one, if they survive the thousand perils threatening the existence of a negative: human carelessness, fire, and all the changes that technique is bound to bring into film production.

A film worthy of the name encounters the same obstacles as does a canvas by Vermeer, Van Gogh or Cézanne. But whilst these paintings land in the public museum only after a long time, a film must begin in it. Thrown to the crowd, it gets classed, and from then on can only count on being seen by a few individuals, similar to the few who saw the paintings when they first appeared, before the eye and mind had grown accustomed to them. In short, a painting that isn't worth a penny to begin with will be worth millions later on. Whereas a film that was worth millions at the start will survive, if at all, in dire poverty.

A.F. After these generalities on cinematography, will you allow me to ask you a more personal question? And will you promise to give me an exhaustive answer? Can you tell me the deep motives that brought you, first among the poets, to an art which most writers despise— even though we observe that they despise it less and less as time goes on?

J.C. Before I reply to the main part of your question, I will say that these writers have a good excuse. Film making is a manual art, a craftsman's job. A work written by one man and then transposed on to the screen by another is no more than a translation, and can, indeed, be of very little interest for a genuine writer (or be of interest only to his pocket). Before film art can be worthy of a writer, the writer must become worthy of film art. I mean, he should not be content with leaving some left-handed work of his to be interpreted by other people, but should seize hold of it with both his hands and work hard at building an object in a style equivalent to his written style. A desk-and-pen man is naturally quite uninterested in films, and doesn't even value them as a means of propagating his ideas. And now let us go back to the personal problems you raised.

1. I am a draughtsman. It is quite natural for me to see and hear what I write, to endow it with a plastic form. When I am shooting a film, every scene I direct is for me a moving drawing, a painter's grouping of material. In Venice, you cannot look at a canvas by Tiepolo or Tintoretto without being struck by its 'stage-setting' and by the deliberate singularity of planes, which goes so far as to allow a leg to protrude beyond the frame, in the bottom left-hand corner. (I'm not quite sure if it is in Tintoretto's Christ asleep in the boat, in the storm, but I think it is.) This method forces me to work in France where we still have disorder and even

anarchy, to some extent. The severity of trade-union regulation in Hollywood and London makes it impossible to work without the intermediary of an army of specialists. But in France, film-making is a family affair, and no one rebels if his prerogatives are encroached upon—lighting, sets, costumes, make-up, music and so forth. All this rests in my hands, and I work in close collaboration with my assistants. Consequently, as my unit itself admits, the film becomes a thing of my very own to which they have contributed by their advice and skill.

2. Film-making isn't my profession. Nothing compels me to direct film after film, to chase after actors for a particular story or vice versa. That would have been a serious handicap. It is much easier to make a film from time to time, when you are seized by the imperative urge to make one, than to be ceaselessly driven to hunt for books and plays, and while you shoot one film to rack your brains over the problems of the next.

3. I sometimes wonder whether my perpetual malaise is not due to my incredible indifference towards the things of this world; whether my work is not a struggle to seize for myself the things that occupy other people; whether my kindness is not a ceaseless effort to overcome my lack of contact with my fellow-men.

Unless I happen to become the vehicle of an

unknown force, which I then clumsily help to take shape, I cannot read, or write, or even think. This vacuum is terrifying. I fill it up as best I can, as one sings in the dark. Besides, my medium-like stupidity affects an air of intelligence which makes my blunders pass for subtle cunning, and my sleepwalker's stumbling for the agility of an acrobat.

It isn't likely that this secret will ever come to light, and I shall probably continue to suffer after my death from a misunderstanding similar to that which makes my life so difficult.

When I have manual work to do, I like to think that I take part in earthly things, and I put all my strength into it like a drowning man clinging to a wreck. This is why I took up film-making, where every minute is occupied by work which shields me from the void where I get lost.

When I say I don't have ideas, I mean that I have embryos of ideas of which I'm not the master; and that I can start on a task only if instead of having an idea, an idea has me, and haunts, disturbs, torments me so unbearably that I am forced to get it out, to rid myself of it at any cost. Thus, work for me is a kind of torture. When this is finished, idleness becomes another kind of torture. And in the vacuum that comes back I feel that I shall never work again.

A.F. Wouldn't these alternations between creative fever and emptiness account for your periodic changes of residence, your moving to and fro between Paris and the country?

J.C. I try to get away from cities because while I'm in them I don't lead a city life. All I get are its disadvantages. But these disadvantages give me an illusion of an active life. Away from towns the void is undisguised. I roam aimlessly about the house and find myself on the stairs or in my bedroom without knowing why I came there. In other words, I don't find my equilibrium either in a crowd or in solitude. My sole recourse—the only game in which I can fool myself by running after a ball—is conversation. Conversation allows me to delude myself. I then flatter myself that I am capable of something without any assistance from an unknown force. I believe that I am free, and I squander that freedom in endless chatter, like a man running faster and faster because he is afraid. But as soon as I am left alone, the lighting changes. I ask myself whether I have betrayed some secrets that were not mine, fatuously pulled to pieces some mysterious mechanism, and brought down upon myself the thunders of the unknown force of which I am the servant but pretended to be the master. My shame becomes a new cause of anguish and fear. I always feel like that after the departure of people with whom I was most at ease.

A.F. The discomfort of silence and that of intercourse with people are not the only ones you have to suffer. There are also your frequent illnesses, although they don't seem to hamper your activity. Pascal would say that you have 'turned them to good account'.

J.C. People were surprised and even shocked because in the *Journal de la Belle et la Bête** and in *Difficulté d'Etre* I dwelt at length on a very painful skin trouble. But it should be understood that for me illness became an occupation of every second and took the place of contacts. It made me a feeling human being instead of an unfeeling ghost. It humanized me and allowed me to take up one of those activities (such as hunting) in which people indulge for amusement. I suffer, therefore I am. That accounts for my lack of modesty. The second stage was: I am, therefore I think. And in order to prove my humanity I had to begin thinking instead of losing myself in a kind of painless sleep.

I live intensely only in dreams. My dreams are detailed, terribly realistic. They involve me in innumerable adventures, in contact with places and people who don't exist in a waking

* Translated as *Beauty and the Beast: Diary of a Film* and reprinted by Dover.

state and who are made up for me by the phenomenon of dreaming down to the smallest object, the smallest gesture and the smallest word. I try to rub it all out in the morning, dreading to confuse the two worlds and add the incomprehensible to the incomprehensible.

Naturally enough, I have no fear of death which seems to me a haven. And on the other hand, as I have no sense of time, I mix up the years of my life and all my landmarks, referring to the day before something that happened many years back, never knowing in what order my various works were born, forgetting entire periods of my life but remembering with wonderful clearness, minute details impossible to place in any definite time—I naturally feel caught in a kind of deadly game of blind-man's-buff in which I stagger about, blindfolded, hands vaguely dangling in front of me, amid derisive laughter.

We tend to forget that as we grow older our system, that is, our creative mechanism, inevitably undergoes disturbances which make its functioning more difficult. We gain in blackness, and mistake it for wisdom. We lose vivacity. The miseries disfiguring our faces don't affect our appearance alone. I imagine that the vehicle of the occult forces that inhabit us, the vehicle that enables us to bring some night into the light of day, must make these forces less and less desirous to express themselves through its intermediary. They dig themselves deep into us and hibernate, as it were. The vehicle loses the suppleness of nerves and muscles that made the enigmatic passage from thought to action possible. The fear of action, as Freud called it, from which most poets suffer, turns into a *sclerosis of action*, and this sclerosis is aggravated by the voice of our professional conscience warning us that we may prove unworthy of our intimate darkness and serve it badly.

A.F. Listening to you and watching you live, I have realized that nothing can be farther removed from the work of a poet than the romantic 'vagueness of the soul'. It doesn't seem that boredom can be called your forte, any more than stupidity.

J.C. Boredom, the shapeless monster whose ravages I observed all around me, was something I had never known myself. I was surprised that people could be bored, I wondered how it was possible. But then, all of a sudden, I saw its smooth face which it is useless to question since it refuses to reply. I came to know it through excessive activity during the intervals of which I was plunged into inactivity. That inactivity had previously been my rhythm and had been filled with ideas and action. But human nature is so constituted that it becomes intoxicated by any kind of speed, and such intoxication by activity (by making a film, for instance) requires a disintoxication as slow and painful as that of an opium smoker. One's hands are empty, they hang limp and won't hold the pen. Writing seems irksome to one who has been climbing ladders, directing actors, giving orders to a team of electricians. This is why my present therapeutic treatment consists in cutting out the bustle, which shakes the wine and prevents it from settling in the bottle. The thing to do is to go back to secrecy, to books that only a few people read, to poems that express the uttermost ends of solitude. I make my way from one state to the other through contacts, through conversation, through a gymnasium where the spirit can readjust itself to living without intermediaries. This is why I am talking to you now and find in it a remedy against that abominable, shameful disease—boredom, with its cortège of 'what's the use? what'll I do? where shall I go?' which drives one straight into disaster.

As I have mentioned dreams, I should point out that film work as I understand it, that is, starting at dawn and going on late into the night without a single minute's pause—for even while I'm eating lunch with my unit I speak about the film—that work, as I was saying, is so compact and takes one so far away from the world and its ways that it comes to resemble dreaming in that the people and the happenings of the film become the only things that matter; so much so that one ceases seeing or hearing anything of what's going on in the outside world, just as a sleeper is too absorbed by the life of his dream to notice when real life enters his bedroom in the form of the morning paper, a letter or a friend. Awakening is exceedingly painful, and all film workers know the wretchedness of the last minutes of a film, when those who have lived for some time together disperse in different directions. It is no doubt the memory of that dream that seizes hold of us when we are alone and drives us back to the strange hurly-burly which we seemed to reject with all our being while it lasted. It is the very opposite of fatigue. A tired man wants to sleep and to dream. A man who is resting looks back to that active dream, cinematography.

A.F. I imagine that films, which have the advantage of going everywhere, must have brought you more contacts and more understanding than your poems and books, which owing to quick sales combined with slow reprinting, are, alas, practically unobtainable.

J.C. Yes, in one sense. No, in another. Famous doesn't mean well known. To be famous and unknown permits one to be *discovered*. The remote audiences which know only my name and a few rumours about me go to see my films which, in spite of the dialogue, are a kind of Esperanto by virtue of the visual style which I already mentioned, the style of images.

Many years ago, as I was glancing through a catalogue of jokes for parties and weddings, I saw the item, 'An object difficult to pick up'. I haven't the slightest idea what that 'object' is or what it looks like, but I like knowing that it exists and I like thinking about it.

A work of art should also be 'an object difficult to pick up'. It must protect itself from vulgar pawing, which tarnishes and disfigures it. It should be made of such a shape that people don't know which way to hold it, which embarrasses and irritates the critics, incites them to be rude, but keeps it fresh. The less it's understood, the slower it opens its petals, the later it will fade. A work of art must make contact, be it even through a misunderstanding, but at the same time it must hide its riches, to reveal them little by little over a long period of time. A work that doesn't keep its secrets and surrenders itself too soon exposes itself to the risk of withering away, leaving only a dead stalk.

Voltaire's plays are a typical example of such a triumph of the immediate, of those flowers completely opened up which fade the next morning. Mademoiselle Clairon, who seems a lucid person, speaks of her Racine parts with pleasure, but shows real enthusiasm only over her Voltaire parts. Racine is still played. Nobody plays Voltaire any more.

Nietzsche wrote (in *The Joyous Wisdom*, if I'm not mistaken): 'Between glory and honours, you must choose; if you want glory, give up honours.' This is because honours go to the visible, whereas beauty is almost invisible, it curls up and is sparing of its breath. A film made by us imposes our presence, commenting on our work without betraying it, and prevents us from losing contact with those who may understand us.

The unknown that I am is glad to be unknown, and suffers from it only in the pitiful moments when a man feels the need of contacts and warmth. That is our mud oozing out. As soon as the soul regains its equilibrium, it is glad to possess deep sound cellars where the wine can settle. At its bad moments, it will dream of orgies at which that wine will flow, intoxicating everybody. In those moments, what increases its loneliness is the knowledge that most men live only by the immediate, and perceive the immediate alone. An evening of good hearty dust in one's eyes will always prevail against an evening calling for meditation and looking into one's own self.

I was delighted to hear that a number of

people returned to see *Orphée* (as much as five or six times), to the amazement of the managements. This is significant, for the cinema is usually regarded as a place where one drops in for a little entertainment as one would for a glass of beer.

This is why film societies, those Courts of Appeal, have so important a part to play, and why they deserve all the support we can give them. This is why I accepted nomination as President of the Fédération des Cinéclubs. But, alas, even film societies are sometimes unable to retrieve old films, which the industrial squall sweeps away in order to clear a space for new ones. We had imagined that great actresses like Greta Garbo would be granted the privilege which was denied to a Rachel or a Sarah Bernhardt. But we were wrong. Today it is impossible to show Garbo in *The Lady of the Camelias*, for instance, to the young people who could not see the film when it came out, for all the copies have been meticulously destroyed. *The Lady of the Camelias* is to be remade with new stars and new methods, using all the latest technical inventions, colour, three dimensions, and what not. It is real disaster. Mrs B., the head of the New York Film Library, finds herself confronted with the same difficulties as Langlois of the Cinémathèque Française whenever she endeavours to save a film from oblivion.

She finds that she cannot obtain a single copy. Chaplin alone escapes that terrible destruction, because he is his own firm and consequently would not fall victim to the perpetual clearing. It is none the less true that fabulous sums are demanded for the showing of any one of his films, and if his very early films are still available it is because the present destructive legislation had not come into force when they were made. This is why René Clair demands the passing of a law of copyright deposit.

A.F. Shall we pass on, if you don't mind, to a detailed account of your activity in films? I'd like to take it in chronological order. So let us begin by *Le Sang d'un Poète*.

J.C. The fact that I let twenty years elapse between that film, my first, and the others, shows that I regarded it as something rather like a drawing or a poem—a drawing or a poem so expensive that I couldn't contemplate making more than one. You realize how rare is a Maecenas prepared to give a poet the chance to express himself in visual terms. And, mind you, the million I spent at the time is the equivalent of a hundred millions today. It is quite wrong to speak about the scale of prices. *One* remains one, and *one hundred* is always one hundred. Nobody, nowadays would give a hundred millions to a young man in order that he may express himself as he pleases. This happened only to Buñuel and to myself, and we are both deeply grateful to this day to the Vicomte de Noailles. With Buñuel, this gratitude goes so far that he puts up without protest with the negative of his film, *L'Age d'or*, being put on the shelf, *L'Age d'or* having created in our patron's circle as much scandal as my own film. But all this happened many years ago. Today, *Le Sang d'un Poète* is considered a surrealist film, whilst in fact it stood in opposition to that movement (which at that time had barely been christened). And the day before yesterday Buñuel was telling me that abroad *Le Sang d'un Poète* is sometimes attributed to him, and *Le Chien Andalou* to me. In other words, his style and mine, so opposed in their day, appear so similar as to be mistaken for each other. In books about the seventh art one often reads that I was influenced by Buñuel, but this is quite absurd, for we shot our films simultaneously and very far from one another, and I saw *Le Chien Andalou* only later, when Buñuel and I had become friends. At this point of our dialogue (which seems to be turning into a monologue) I should like to remind you that in New York *Le Sang d'un Poète* has been running for the past fifteen years at the same cinema. It is the longest run ever known. Outside France, *Le Sang d'un Poète* and *Le Chien Andalou* are shown over and over again, and I suppose *L'Age d'or* would be performed just as often if it weren't for Buñuel's scruples. For all that, no company today would take the risk of making films of that kind (as their rarity goes to prove), even though none of the so-called commercial films produced by these competent men have ever reached that number of performances. They always answer you by saying that those are exceptional cases, and they seem quite incapable of imagining that such exceptions may occur again in other forms.

A.F. What about *Orphée?*

J.C. *Orphée* (which is an orchestration made twenty years later, of the theme which in *Le Sang d'un Poète* was clumsily played with one finger) has already provoked the following remark from a producer who was astonished by its takings: 'Nowadays, all you have to do to make money is walk on your head. It's not difficult.' Well, let him try.

A.F. How did you succeed in making the film, in the face of this basic opposition?

J.C. I'll tell you about that later. But I was certainly fully aware of the risk we were taking, my actors and myself. The film was made possible only by their generosity, which led them to accept as payment the promise of a percentage of future takings. And the overspending which I was unable to avoid while we were working on location in the ruins of the Saint-

Cyr barracks (where we had to do some night shooting which required the use of electric generators) I covered out of my own pocket. A film like *Orphée* can by a miracle turn out to be a good investment, but it doesn't look like one at the beginning, and it was made quite outside the usual machinery of the film industry. With *Le Sang d'un Poète*, the Vicomte de Noailles gave it to us (Auric and myself) as a present. But *Orphée* has to refund the millions advanced by the Crédit National and the distributors. It is only after that that we'll get anything out of it. I will speak to you about the film itself in due course, but I thought it worth while to record the countless obstacles we have to overcome before the first shot can be made, even when our names seem to inspire confidence.

A.F. Well, shall we speak about that first shot? I'm sure you will be surprised by my memory: I still remember, having had the pleasure of knowing you for the last twenty-six years, your first attempt at film-making. You were very absorbed by it at the time. That attempt, which preceded *Le Sang d'un Poète* by several years, you undertook singlehanded, *en dilettante*, almost as a kind of escapade. We laughed a lot about it, you and I. What adventures you had! Or, rather, what mis-adventures! They made such an amusing story that you decided at one point to call the film, if it were ever shown at all, '*Jean Cocteau fait du Cinema*', in the style of Chaplin's films of that period, '*Charlot patine*', etc. Best of all, there was that incredible studio, Studio des Cigognes, run by a lady. I also remember how, groping already then for the style which was to become that of *Le Sang d'un Poète*, you draped your actors in wet sheets; these sheets were dipped in hot water; but while they waited between shots, the unfortunate actors, one after another, caught bronchitis. As for yourself, the vicious lighting made you blind for three days. And that isn't the whole story. . . . But in the end what became of that film that nobody, not even your friends, has ever seen?

J.C. I know that Pierre Bromberger has been trying to track it down for some time, but I don't know what the outcome will be. The wave that sweeps away whatever I possess has also swept the only copy of that film. There seems to be no trace of it anywhere. As to the lady director of the Studio des Cigognes, I wonder what has become of her. She was very odd. One day the electric lights weren't working, and I asked her what was wrong. She said, 'I've put the handles down, so we'll just have to wait for the electricity to come through.'

A.F. I mentioned your idea of naming your

film *à la* Charlie Chaplin. You must have admired Chaplin already at that time?

J.C. Yes, I admired Chaplin's films, as well as Buster Keaton's, which are now quite impossible to get hold of (there was one in particular with a lot of Chinese), and Harry Langdon's. Langdon brought ruin to all his producers because the American public found his humour lugubrious. All that is left of them are a few 16-mm. films belonging to Henri Filippachi with whom I made a film myself last year. It's *Coriolan*, a 16-mm. film which very possibly will remain as unknown as the Cigognes film.

A.F. Why do you think that?

J.C. Because we shot it in the country in two Sundays, with the few people who happened to be present. I play in it with Jean Marais, Josette Day and a dressmaker's dummy we found among some studio props and brought along with us, around which the whole film revolves.

A.F. I fail to see how such a cast can prevent the film being shown.

J.C. There's something else. Filippachi, to whom the camera and the projector belonged, has a mania for machines and for fishing. I suppose he is guarding that frightful document like a treasure, and shows it in small doses. Rossellini has seen it and likes it very much. I called it *Coriolan* because I appear in it as an old man shooting eagles to the accompaniment of the overture of *Coriolanus*. Moreover, I suspect that Filippachi is afraid that this piece of Sunday fun may be taken too seriously. It would be lamentable if this tragic toy were to become a pretext for ciné-club battles. Needless to say, the mystery in which it is enveloped adds to its attraction, and I keep getting offers for it from all over the world, at any price. But why should I accept? It is a rare luxury in our days to be the owner of an invisible work of art which one day may become extremely interesting.

A.F. So from your Cigognes films to your most recent one, the 'dilettante' loops the loop, since the 16-mm. film is a dilettante method. Don't you think that 16-mm. could be extremely useful for the young people of today who cannot hope to be backed by rich art patrons?

J.C. The answer I'll give you now won't be the one I would have given you some months ago. For I have realized since then that a 16-mm. film can be very expensive, even more expensive, in proportion, than a real film, since it is made without any support from the outside. Moreover, what I call 'a 16-mm.' is really a film made 'in the 16-mm. spirit'. A few young friends of mine who started shooting a film with 16-mm. stock, re-shot what they had shot and continued on 35-mm. They noticed then that there was not much difference in cost, and that the ruinous expenses come from the studio, the stars, the sets, all of which you can do without if you have a cellar and a few lamps. What I find very sad is that the innumerable 16-mm. films I've seen either imitate commercial films or plunge headlong into experiments which were legitimate for us but are now out of date. In America, on the other hand, many young people use the 16-mm. medium to express themselves as freely as if they were in a psychiatrist's consulting room. The result is remarkably interesting, and I feel that if everybody came out with such confessions, the camera would produce works as fascinating as those written in solitude. I'd like to use this opportunity to beseech our innumerable amateurs to resist the lure of technique, to stop playing at professional film-makers, and not to be afraid of being bold or even mad. Otherwise they will have nothing to show except second-rate cinema which hasn't yet found its true register. They have more freedom than we have. They must not waste it.

A.F. Here again, you show them the way

with *Coriolan*. Excuse my harping on it, but was the film prepared in advance?

J.C. Absolutely not. We made it up as we went, using the possibilities as they cropped up. The film begins with credits longer than the film itself, introducing the producers, the backer, the cameraman, the still photographer and the cast. Incidentally the photographer is not the photographer. It is Georges Huguet, who happened to be there. The backer isn't the backer. It is the owner of the restaurant 'Le Catalan', and so on. Filippachi and myself are seen perusing countless volumes which, needless to say, have nothing whatsoever to do with the film. As to the subtitles (for nothing interests me more than the *accidental synchronism* of which I will speak to you later on), I took them out of a documentary on basket-making and stuck them under our pictures. . . . But haven't we spoken long enough about *Coriolan*?

All this, you might say, is a Sunday hoax, surprising at our age. I can reply by quoting Picasso. Somebody once accused him of being a mystifier, and he replied that all the great painters had been mystifiers, meaning that all great painters gave their answers long before the questions had been posed, and thereby mystified their contemporaries. One shouldn't be afraid of playing pranks. They denote a state of spiritual relaxation, when oddities spring up almost spontaneously, without the shadow of an effort. Such is the case with children's *mots* and children's answers in American intelligence tests—which only a genius would have been able to make up as a grown-up and in cold blood.

Alain Fournier, when he was teaching in a primary school, once asked a little girl to describe a cow. Answer: 'The cow is a big animal with four legs that go right down to the ground.'

American intelligence test: A little girl is asked to describe the winter. 'In winter,' she says, 'the forest is made of wood.' Another question: 'Name the circulatory organs.' Answer: 'Feet.' To the question, 'Who was Penelope?' a little boy replies: 'Penelope was Ulysses' last trial after his travels.'

I could cite you a thousand more, in the vein of *The Young Visitors*, where little Daisy Ashford describes the Queen of England as wearing 'a small but costly crown'. Could it be better said? And when she heard about the Crystal Palace, she imagined something strange and wonderful, comparable to the court-room of Kafka's *Trial* or to Lewis Carroll's scenery.

A.F. From some remarks you made about yourself, and from your interest in children's sayings, I gather that you are preoccupied with the question of age. Quite disinterestedly, for what matters for you is to continue to be productive. Does this feeling of 'sclerosis' of action disturb you in your work?

J.C. Yes, often, and much more than the refusals I keep coming up against, which are quite natural since France is in a way my 'family', and one is always nagged by one's family. I've got to the point of never telling that family of mine about my successes abroad, for France would answer with the words of the mother in *Les Parents Terribles*: 'Outside, people praise you and flatter you, so when I tell you what you really are . . .'

A.F. This comes from the bewildering complexity of your work. Would you say, on the whole, that you are unfairly treated?

J.C. It is not unfairness I'm up against, or hatred or intrigues. It is a *conspiracy of noise*, similar to a conspiracy of silence. It is as though the difficulty of seizing hold of my work, of pinning me down, exasperates the critics to screaming point. That screaming has become a reflex. It has taken the place of study. People shrink from study. Instead they take a short cut and they scream. That screaming may seem unkind and insulting, but I'm never offended by it, for it reminds me of the laughter with which an audience expresses its feelings of surprise, even when this is of a tragic nature, simply because laughter and tears are the only two ways in which they are capable of expressing their feelings. I seldom open a newspaper without its screaming out at me, in mockery or anger. I imagine that breaking out of that acquired rhythm would require an effort rather like the one it takes to stop a hiccup. And it would be absurd to expect such an effort from someone accustomed to thinking and writing too fast, on the corner of a café table or on his knee in the theatre. I know that somewhere in the shade there are a few young people who are exasperated by that hiccup and who sit down to study my work. Their day will come when the hiccup is gone and when fatigue changes the conspiracy of noise into a conspiracy of silence. Then they will have a chance to speak up.

Besides, every man is born either slapped or a slapper. There are some people of whom it will always be said that they've been slapped, even when it was they that did the slapping; and others of whom one says that they slapped someone when in fact they had been slapped themselves. I belong to the first race. I was born slapped, which makes things very easy for impostors, because I am too lazy to hit back, and everybody knows it and takes advantage of it. If I am robbed, I just let the thief go, preferring him to the policeman. And, after all, it was my fault. I had no business to fall for his tricks and let him in, and leave him alone in my room. In the conspiracy of noise that surrounds me, there is also a conspiracy of silence. This conspiracy of silence comes from the friends who never speak of you just when they should have done, when mentioning your name would have been useful because it would assert your presence in a manner more alive and warmer than can be done by the conspiracy of noise. Radio gives us an instance of that. The people who speak on it don't think that you may be listening, and consequently they choose to forget you, even though what they say calls for a mention of your name, a reference to your work.

A.F. I agree that noise is one of the calamities of our time, but you are not the only one to be affected by it. It is extremely disagreeable for everybody. The radio, for instance, adds to the general din, violating our most intimate solitude.

J.C. Yes. In the past, the artist was face to face with silence. Today, that silence makes a frightful noise. Everybody interferes with everything. It is the fault of the Encyclopaedists. Funnily enough, they were the first to complain that they were judged by pastry cooks (Diderot mentions this). But it was they who killed the élite, proclaiming that everybody had the right to think. As a result, in 1951 even the stupid think. That is something that has never happened before. A Parisian audience considers that it can write better than the author and act better than the actors. We have no public any more, we have only judges. An individualistic crowd, a crowd unfit for the collective hypnosis without which a spectacle becomes pointless. But this resistance ceases as soon as a mass audience pours in. They've paid for their seats and they are determined to enjoy the show. So it is not the mass audience that I accuse, but the false élite that has planted itself between the masses and ourselves. This false élite, which lives only by fashion, decrees that a work is out of fashion as soon as it deviates from what it considers fashionable. Yes, indeed! It is out of fashion like everything that matters, everything that refuses to obey the dictates of stupidity.

The difference is that in 1930 this public was shocked. In 1951, it despises. It has taken the upper hand. It is a jury. What would become of us if there were not a higher court, that of the masses and the foreign audiences, which do not hear about our petty disputes until much later?

A.F. I dare say you include in that general din the discordant voices of the critics. But let's try to be fair. Is there any particular critic whose opinions you would consider more valid than the rest?

J.C. Léautaud might have been that critic. But he doesn't view films. At the theatre, when he liked a play he spoke about it. When he disliked it he spoke about his cats. That's the way to do it.

A.F. Do you like Léautaud?

J.C. Yes. Marie Laurencin says, 'He's sky blue.' It's true. He is sky blue; in spite of his cape, his soft felt hat, his walking stick, his woollen muffler, he looks like a pastel drawing by Liotard. He is a man of the eighteenth century, a dream Encyclopaedist, as Mallarmé would have said. A magical Encyclopaedist. Pity he isn't one of our judges.

A.F. You haven't much love for the race of judges?

J.C. You know what Jean Genêt has said of Gide? 'He is on the side of the judges, but leans amorously towards the accused.' He refused to meet Gide. 'His immorality,' he said, 'looks pretty fishy to me.'

A.F. What do you think of Genêt's work?

J.C. I admire him as a fabulist. He makes animals talk. I mean, men who have no language, whose feelings are so complex that they cannot express them.

A.F. But what do you think of him as a thief?

J.C. Colette says I'm no good as an idler. Genêt is no good as a thief. Theft is just a hobby with him. Sartre and I maintain that this is what accounts for his vogue. Our epoch dotes on crooks and thieves. Hence Maurice Sachs's success.

A.F. Would you care to speak to me about Maurice Sachs?

J.C. No. I think well of him but would speak ill. I'd rather pass on to some other game.

A.F. Just one more word about Genêt. Hasn't he just made a film?

J.C. Yes, a beautiful film in which he uses the visual language with the greatest ease. But it is very difficult to see that film.

A.F. I should like to return to you. Tell me, after all you said about judges, is it possible for you to take up the position of a critic in front of your own work?

J.C. Writing a book is not the same as reading it. Producing a play is not the same as seeing it.

This calls for some leniency in judging our judges. We can't expect them to assimilate in two hours a spectacle that took us quite a time to make out. A work of art, once it has detached itself from us, begins to live according to its readers or its audiences, who distort it for their own use. And we ourselves undergo a transformation and change into the readers or spectators of a work which at that moment we would be incapable of creating. We look at it from the outside, and it surprises us. We become its critics. And it becomes impossible for us to change anything whatsoever in it. We see its errors, but we can't correct them. This is because the worst is of the same fabric as the best, and these threads are so closely interwoven that by pulling at one we risk destroying the lot. It is from such an amalgam that beauty is born. Too much cleaning can kill the microbes and the rotten tissues of which life is composed. There have been cases in America of women dying from excessive purging, for what they drove out of their systems was the very principle of life, which rests on vermin, however unflattering this statement may sound. In any case, no works of mine have ever been seriously studied, or examined in relation to one another. I've merely been pounced upon at every turn and accused of being light. I am that, certainly, and I'm proud of it. But it isn't the kind of

lightness they are thinking of. Lightness consists in judging a work lightly, without taking
its roots into account. Every work of art has its
secret places, and one may wonder which is
best, to discover them or leave them undiscovered. Rimbaud is devoured by lice. One rids
him of a few, and gives him others. Only spirit
rappers question a table. Never a joiner, who
handles it and judges it as a table.* The ideal
is to be famous, unknown and undiscovered.

It is strange to think that if we followed the
advice of the critics, the journalists and practically all our contemporaries, those very contemporaries would turn away from us and would
deny us even the small importance which now
makes them take some interest in our persons.
For what makes them grant us that importance
is precisely the secret force in us which they
reject and which they urge us to renounce. That
force is what gives us presence—a presence they
perceive but whose reasons they are incapable
of analysing. They think that we are present by
some sort of mistake or accident, and that
thanks to their guidance and advice this mistake can be put right, and our accidental presence can become a solid and legitimate position.
And we shall then come to some good instead of
going to the bad.

* Goffin's book, *Verlaine et Rimbaud*, is a study of the
table.

A.F. It is none the less true that in exposing something one exposes one's self. It seems to me that a creator cannot claim the privilege of anonymity or the comforts of solitude.

J.C. This doesn't apply only to films. One doesn't write for oneself, either. This would be quite absurd. If one did, it would suffice merely to think; and even thinking would be too much. It would suffice to *be* a silent masterpiece. We write for the non-existent reader who might understand us better than we do ourselves. Those who approve of us bear some resemblance to that reader, though a remote one, rather like a rough sketch. It is a vague family resemblance.

A.F. Have you ever had occasion to observe such a family likeness?

J.C. Yes, in innumerable letters. A film reputed difficult and non-commercial (that is, considered such in film circles), if it epitomises an artist whose other works are not very well known, can be compared to a huge edition of a poet's book. Naturally, such a book will fall from many a reader's hands. But it multiplies our chances of reaching perceptive people whom in the past an artist never reached, or very rarely, and sometimes only after he was dead. The letters I just mentioned bear this out. They never correspond to the hasty articles of our judges, and don't take the slightest notice of them.

We mustn't forget our main privilege, which comes from the mechanism of change. One franc is now a thousand francs, and one person is a thousand people. The level, mind you, hasn't changed, and if Baudelaire's twelve listeners at his lecture in Brussels are now twelve thousand, their understanding is none the greater for that. But there is more of everything. I have had time to see this evolution. When I was very young, retailers were few and one dealt with only two or three shops. The periodical *Je Sais Tout* was an event. The newspaper, *Excelsior*, another. There were very few pretty women one knew by name, and very few restaurants where these pretty women could be seen. Very few theatres. Every new book made a sensation when it came out. There were piles of it in every bookshop. A single article could make or break a man, and so on and so forth. But to *hold out* today in the midst of the innumerable is very difficult. And *holding out* has become the real problem, in France and everywhere else. For forty years now I've been holding out. If what the critics have been saying about me were true, you'll agree that I wouldn't have been able to hold out. My meeting with Picasso in 1916 was my great lesson. He was for all of us an example of hidden continuity, the only one of which one never tires, and which one notices only in retrospect and from a certain angle. Just like Holbein's dead head: if you look at it sideways and from a distance it is just a conglomeration of blobs. Some tiling is like that, presenting one pattern till the eye suddenly perceives another. After that it is very difficult to come back to one's first vision. Patience, for us, means being prepared to wait for that new angle of vision. This being so, how can we be content with making films which we know will be killed by technical progress? Inevitably, we use films exclusively as means of deep personal propaganda. But on the other hand, it is quite understandable that films should be generally regarded as the art of our epoch, since that epoch naïvely believes that it, too, is denied a future, and that Europe is old, whereas in fact it must be very young, seeing that the earth itself, in terms of human life, is something like seventeen years old, the age of rows and brawls.

A.F. If I have understood you rightly, you belong to those who believe in the durability of things on our planet?

J.C. And yet I very seldom lose sight of the fact that we are on a ball whirling round at top speed and that the whole thing is in a matrix which has the regrettable tendency to distend.

A.F. Doesn't this—what shall I call it?—cosmic philosophy depress you and hinder your work? Doesn't it give you a kind of 'what's the use' feeling?

J.C. Quite the contrary. It makes our human scale all the more precious to me. That great mystery makes me modest and attentive to small tasks.

A.F. Too modest . . .

J.C. No. Shakespeare himself did a small job compared to the greatness of the universe. And since our little ball is liable to explode or freeze or what have you, how can we be offended by a critic's rebuke?

A.F. At this point, I feel that I must interrupt the monologue of a man in the clutches of his dæmon and, with all due respect, lead you back to the precise little facts which, incidentally, you like. Tell me: when you discovered the world of films, coming as you did from quite another world, what did it have to offer that was entirely *new* to you?

J.C. My big discovery was that the cinematograph was the refuge of craftsmanship. In our days, craftsmen are regarded as the aristocracy of the working classes. There is a tendency to do away with craftsmanship. But on the studio floor, the technicians are craftsmen in the strictest sense of the term, particularly in France where individual resourcefulness and inventiveness still have their place. The impossible becomes possible thanks to the *genius* (in the Stendhalian sense of the word) of the French worker, for whom a problem is a challenge, and who always finds some makeshift solution. The deficiencies of our film equipment help that genius to survive, in an epoch bent on destroying it. The studio floor is the last stronghold of feudalism, where people spare no pains to please the master—a master not in any imperialist sense of the term, but rather like the master-builder of the days of the cathedrals, who worked as hard as his men. (This makes all the difference, so that the word 'feudal' is probably misleading.) When I work on a film I'm the first to arrive and the last to leave, and I never show the slightest sign of tiredness. During the shooting of *La Belle et la Bête*, it was my unit, electricians, studio-hands and others, who refused to go on working, saying that I was killing myself, and who ordered me, as it were, to leave Saint-Maurice and let myself be taken to the Hôpital Pasteur. If we try to analyse this attitude, we'll see that it was not a case of taking advantage of my illness to snatch a holiday, but that they were defending the progress of our common work and that they were devoted to that work and to me. I've never yet come across a film director who speaking of his unit did not affirm, 'It's the best there is.' This brings me back to the idea of a Family, which has nothing in common with the family from which all its members disperse, but is akin to the family (or the village) of antiquity, bound by a common interest and by that affectionate attachment which grows from contact—a attachment which is dead in our modern society where contacts no longer take place.

A.F. I have once witnessed an extreme instance of such a contact brought about by your work, without your knowledge and almost against your will. I heard one evening a personal enemy of yours recite by heart one of your poems, which, he said, he regarded as the most beautiful in the whole of modern poetry, while in his articles he attacks you every day.

J.C. That makes me think of a fraternity of a higher order, akin to that of the initiated of a secret lodge. I am thinking of the bond of deep friendship that exists in our days between men who create completely different works of art, even though their respective admirers are convinced that they must hate each other. You know, for instance, what Orson Welles thinks of *Orphée*. He is undoubtedly one of its most genuine supporters. And yet a young Orson

Welles fan imagines that his admiration for *Citizen Kane* forbids him to admire *Orphée* as well. The same applies to my friendship with Sartre, and to the friendship between all the other artists who on the surface seem to be in opposition to each other, but who are spiritually united in their total *engagement* to a cause, however different the causes to which they have pledged themselves may be.

A.F. So the famous word is out at last! I won't miss this opportunity to ask what you think of the *engagement* theory.

J.C. Sartre knows what I think of it. My *engagement* is to lose myself in the ultimate, most uncomfortable depths of my being. If I were to 'engage' myself outside as well, I would inevitably betray either my inner or my outer pledge.

In our days a free man passes for a coward, whereas in fact he doesn't secure a single spot where he would be safe from blows. He is stoned from all sides. He is the snow statue of *Le Sang d'un Poète*.

It amuses me to hear my friends François Mauriac and Henry Janseon call me a Communist, just because I happen to sign an occasional article in a Communist paper. Quite apart from the fact that the Communist Party doesn't hesitate to sacrifice even its own members, and that an article coming from an outsider cannot entitle him to expect protection from any quarter, my policy is one of friendship, not of prudence. Between you and me, it looks quite imprudent. But Eluard and Aragon are perfect friends, more perfect than those who reproach me for knowing them. I will remain their friend whatever happens, and if they ask me to write something for them, I'll do so. I am sorry to have to say such obvious things to people for whom the duties of friendship don't seem to count any more. They accuse me of lightness. But in my eyes lightness consists in changing one's attitude according to circumstances. Besides, Giraudoux always said to me: 'Whenever anybody wants to hit us, it's you they hit. You are the ideal lightning-rod that diverts the lightning from us.'

A.F. Please, don't let us drop *Le Sang d'un Poète* just as it lies within our reach. How did you happen to embark on that adventure?

J.C. I didn't know that my position was one of solitude. In those days, politics meant a politics of Letters and Arts, unconnected with politics proper. It was quite different from the present-day situation. And *Le Sang d'un Poète* was an act of politics in that sense, an act of opposition against the surrealist policy, which in those days was all-powerful (particularly so because it was so new). What complicated matters was that the surrealists and I admired the same values and fought on the same level, whilst the present confusion of levels would render all these battles quite incomprehensible. Actually, it's already rendered them incomprehensible, since, as I told you, in South America young people ascribe my films to Luis Buñuel and his to me, under the surrealist label.

A.F. Remembering the films we were being shown at that time, I suppose you meant *Le Sang d'un Poète* to be a gesture of protest?

J.C. No, for I wasn't thinking about making a film. I was merely trying to express myself through a medium which in the past had been inaccessible to poets. So much so that without being aware of it I was portraying myself, which happens to all artists who use their models as mere pretexts. Freud was right when he said about *Le Sang d'un Poète* that it was like peeping through a keyhole at a man who is undressing. There have been innumerable attempts at interpreting *Le Sang d'un Poète*, including even the contention that the film was a detailed account of the history of Christianity. As I was questioning a young philosopher belonging to the group responsible for that exegesis, he said that there was only one thing he found disconcerting, one of the first sentences in the film: 'While the guns

of Fontenay were thundering in the distance. . .'
'Surely,' he said, 'it is at Fontenay that the Eucharistic Congress was held?' And as I protested feebly, he exclaimed, feeling he had hit at last on an irrefutable argument: 'But you can't deny that the dead child's imprint in the snow is that of Veronica's veil?' Another case: three hundred girls of a Roman Catholic centre of psychoanalysis decided that the factory chimney which starts crumbling down at the beginning of the film and finally collapses at the end of it (designed to show that the time of action had the immediate quality of dreams) was a phallic symbol. One half of the critics of *Le Sang d'un Poète* regarded it as an erotic film, and the other half as an icy abstraction devoid of all humanity. It was following these experiences that I said, 'Poetry springs from those who don't worry about it. We are cabinetmakers. The spirit rappers come afterwards and if they care to make our tables speak it's entirely their own business.'

A.F. But you, the joiner, have you any idea of the meaning of *Le Sang d'un Poète?*

J.C. Our thoughts cease being exactly our thoughts as soon as we've written them down. And even while they're still just thoughts, they are already mere phantoms of our beliefs. We write them down to give them flesh and blood.

But we very seldom succeed in giving them a physique, a body corresponding to what they really are. Syntax interferes, and also our creative mania which leads us further and further away from them as we try to embellish them and give them more character. In short, we endow them with a force and an existence which often turn against us.

A.F. Still, while you were shooting *Le Sang d'un Poète*, were you aware of what you were doing?

J.C. No more than a man is aware when he dozes in front of the fire in a semi-conscious state. I did my work just as such a man might poke at the fire while half asleep.

A.F. I notice that in that film, which, in spite of you and in spite of itself, has become the archetype of the *poetic film*, the text that accompanies it is dry, the very opposite of what is termed poetic.

J.C. I wanted to avoid any pleonasm; not to superimpose a poetic text on an image that I already blamed for being poetic in so far as what was seen in it was seen and a sort of realism of the unreal. In other words, that film contained visible proof that the unreal existed as an object, which I actually showed. But on the whole, I'm sure that the lasting success of the film is largely due to my mistakes, and to the possibility I give to the spectators to enter into it and play a part in it. A film more closed, such as *Orphée*, has fewer entrances, so that many people butt against locked doors. And the speed inherent in any cinematic spectacle leaves them no time to try out different keys.

A.F. You have often been blamed for not perpetually re-making *Le Sang d'un Poète*, for having forsaken that singular path.

J.C. This is because by sheer chance *Le Sang d'un Poète* was made at a time when strangeness was recognizable as strangeness, that is to say, it displayed its attributes. But later on our spirit of contradiction (and all creation is the spirit of contradiction in its highest form) caused us to change that visible singularity for invisible singularity, which, unfortunately could only too easily be mistaken for retrogression. This is what happened to *Les Parents Terribles*, a film which in its way and for its time was quite as daring as *Le Sang d'un Poète*. Even more daring, I would say, because its boldness was less obvious.

A.F. Please! I must call you to order. You're muddling up my chronology. *Les Parents Terribles* did not immediately follow *Le Sang d'un Poète*, and for the first film that you made alone you chose a subject which if not poetic is at least fantastic: the fairy-tale about Beauty and the Beast.

J.C. The main reason why I chose it was that the story as I saw it was a fairy-tale without fairies. In the film *La Belle et la Bête*, just as in *L'Eternel Retour*, I noticed that the two passages where poetry is best expressed disappointed many people. In the first film, the sisters in the farm-yard; in the second, the garage. This is because the public expects fairies, or at least, in default of fairies, it expects what in modern parlance is termed *évasion*, escape. But genuine poetry has no use for evasion. What it wants is *invasion*, that is, that the soul be invaded with words and objects which, just because they don't present a winged appearance, impel it to plunge deep into itself. Therefore it's through sheer frivolous laziness that the public prefers poetic poetry, fantastic fairy plays, and rebels against anything that requires a personal effort of fantasy and magic.

A.F. But wasn't that precisely the complaint we heard most frequently about *La Belle et la Bête*—that you imposed your personal mythology on a story that wasn't your own?

J.C. Quite apart from the fact that I chose that particular fable just because it corresponded to my personal mythology, the funny

La Belle et la Bête: Beauty's brother (Michel Auclair) and her haughty sisters (Nane Germon and Mila Parely). (Courtesy Ernest D. Burns of Cinemabilia)

La Belle et la Bête: Beauty (Josette Day) holds the horse for her father, the

part of it all is that the objects and happenings for which I'm held responsible are to be found in a book by Madame Leprince de Beaumont, written in England, where there are countless stories about monsters hidden in old family mansions. It was, precisely, what was *true* in that book that tempted me and led me to the *unreal realism* I have mentioned earlier on.

A.F. In view of the great success the film won with the real public, I wonder if you foresaw, when you adapted that fable, that it would be an answer to an unconscious need?

J.C. I knew it all the less as the first public contact, at the Festival at Cannes, bordered upon disaster. The terrible élite of judges deemed that the film would pass over the heads of children and would seem childish to grown-ups. The film's extraordinary success began only after it jumped that first wall, which we always find in our way and which distressed my producer to such an extent that he implored me to cut out one of the best scenes of the film—but only to ask me, three years later, to put it back.

A.F. That experience might have convinced you that you were offering the public just what it expected from you. Why then did you change?

J.C. Our business is not to obey the public,

65

which doesn't know what it wants, but to compel it to follow us. If it won't come we must use cunning—pictures, stars, *décors* and other magic lanterns apt to intrigue the children and make them swallow what we have to give them. After that they may digest it. Provided they don't instantly eliminate it, the beneficial poison is absorbed into their system. Little by little, the malady of stupidity becomes less virulent, and even in a few rare cases can be completely cured. I have seen a few instances of that.

A.F. I'd like to question you now on some technical points which I think aren't devoid of interest. We all know that a film unfolds itself according to very strict laws and a rigorous order, and that a film creator is not free, in the sense in which a writer is free when he writes a novel or a poem that he can extend or compress at his pleasure. When you were making your *début* in films, didn't you feel trammelled by the rigid timing imposed on you by the exhibitors?

J.C. I must confess that I have never timed a film or a theatre play. We all carry within ourselves, in our guts, like the Negroes one sees in fairgrounds, a clock that wakes us at the appointed time. People often opposed me with figures and the figures proved wrong. Our instinct is surer. I must add that the accepted length of a film, eight to ten thousand feet, is bad. Too short to correspond to a novel and too long to correspond to a short story. In consequence of this, film-making is beset with pitfalls of a different kind from those one finds in other arts.

A.F. But this amounts to an admission that you, too, are sometimes a victim of technique.

J.C. It's very difficult for an active poet to speak of technique, for all his art is made of numbers that can't be expressed in figures, of equilibrium that passes for disequilibrium and order that appears to be disorder. After *Orphée*, Clouzot said: 'That film proves that there's no such thing as technique, but only invention, and that the only possible technique is the one every man invents for himself according to the job he's doing.'

A.F. Before we leave the question of technique —how did you manage to work with collaborators so important and, to all appearances, so capricious as Christian Bérard and Georges Auric? How did you go about it?

J.C. As far as Bérard was concerned, he was both indefatigable and lazy in the extreme. He suffered from what the psychoanalysts call 'fear of action'. I used to take him along with me when I composed a work. His inventions inspired mine. He *told* me the *décors* and costumes.

But as soon as the moment came to draw them he would shy like a horse. I knew the method. So I immediately betrayed him and went ahead behind his back, ordering sketches of *décors* and sketches of costumes to be drawn according to what he had told me. My blunders being more than he could bear, he'd hurl himself on the sketches and start correcting them, sweating and mopping his face in distress. Jouvet would recognize that system, an admirable form of collaboration, which in our case led to a perfect marriage between the setting and the direction.

A.F. Since your collaboration was as close as that, I can assume that for *La Belle et la Bête* you yourself, as well as Bérard, adopted that Dutch atmosphere that I for one found splendid, haunted by memories of Vermeer, Rembrandt and Peter de Hooch, which sets in a very definite place a fairy-tale originally unattached to any country or epoch.

J.C. The idea to give realism and a date to vagueness originated in the house I discovered in Touraine. Tired of hunting for what is known as a location, I was on the point of turning back when Wakhevitch, who was with me, said he had heard about a small property below the level of the road we were about to take. I must confess I was so tired that at first I refused to make that last attempt. But he insisted and I gave in. And as we were walking down the hill from which we could see neither house nor garden, we suddenly heard my voice. *The owner's son was playing my poetry records to his father.* So we were welcomed as a miracle, and as though by a miracle again, we found every architectural detail and all the places which I was afraid we'd have to build. That farm imposed a definite style, and that style determined everything else. And there was even more of a coincidence: all the iron-work of the building was made in the shape of the Beast!

Now, as you mentioned Vermeer and the Dutch School, I'd like to open a parenthesis on painting in films.

The present arrangement of programmes is a disaster. It doesn't give a chance to the short film, a genre which has produced masterpieces in France. Resnais' *Guernica* is one. *Van Gogh* is another. Surprisingly enough, painting, when it is filmed, acquires a new intensity of life. Van Gogh's landscapes, for instance, including those that seem the maddest, *deceive the eye to such an extent that they look like real location shots.* Only when the camera draws quite close to the canvas does one realize that the landscape is painted.

On the other hand, Grémillon has filmed the most mediocre exhibits of the Salon des Artistes Français. And those paintings, being deliberate stage-settings in themselves, lose their ridiculousness and become quite charming. The effect is really unexpected. Their relief and composition suddenly become extremely pleasing. One feels that one would like to have them in one's house. Thus the film puts the painter's honesty to the test. A painting *pretentious in content* is unacceptable on the screen.

A.F. Speaking of Ingres, Degas has said: 'Great painting is smooth.' And this reminds me—thinking of all your metamorphoses as a craftsman—why do people always speak of a 'violon d'Ingres' * whenever someone changes his tools?

J.C. But why shouldn't Ingres have played the violin well? His Thetis' neck is like the bowing of a violin. How I'd love to play the violin as Ingres did!

A.F. Let us go back to your films, and to Christian Bérard.

J.C. His death left me alone for the shooting of *Orphée* after all the preparatory work we'd done together in the country. It was because I couldn't entrust anybody else with the suburban *zone* which he, as well as myself, wanted anti-Dantesque and without any lyricism, that *zone* of which I have a series of gouaches reminiscent

* A hobby. (Transl.)

of the dream streets of the Halle aux Vins (Quai de Bercy), that I did the shooting in the ruins of the Saint-Cyr barracks. Indeed, in my film the places of death are not the Place of Death; and I was very struck by the words of a White Father who said that just as it happens in the immediacy of dreams, that *zone* preceded death and represented the few moments of coma.

A remarkable thing: whenever Bérard displayed any concern about *Orphée*, that concern always went to a character representing one of the innumerable figures of death. He sought ways of making death elegant (in the gravest sense of the word), and used to say with a laugh: 'Everything about death is costly; I ought to know, since my mother was *née* Borniol.'* Bérard's death is an irreparable loss. He was the only man to understand that Wonderland has little use for vagueness, and that mystery exists only in precise things. He also knew that nothing is easier in films than false fantasy. He avoided it with unerring grace.

A.F. Let us now speak of the place you give to music in your films. The score of *La Belle et la Bête* is important, and was composed by Georges Auric as was the music of all your other films.

J.C. Nothing, it seems to me, can be more vulgar than musical synchronism in films. It is,

* A well-known firm of undertakers. (Transl.)

again, a pleonasm. A kind of lime where everything gets stuck rigid, and where no play (in the sense of 'play' in wood) is possible. What I like is accidental synchronism, the effectiveness of which I have had occasion to observe again and again. The best example I can cite comes from a ballet, not a film—*Le Jeune Homme et la Mort* where at the very last moment I decided to use Bach's *Passacaglia* so as to make the dances, based on jazz rhythms, take on an unexpected grandeur. Already from the second performance on, the dancers 'inclined' towards the music, the conductor 'inclined' towards the dancers, and everything fell into place, so well, alas, that people refused to believe that the choreography had not been based on Bach.

A.F. But how can you hope for such accidental synchronism occurring with a score specially composed for a particular film?

J.C. I provoke it. Very often Auric gets annoyed, but he always ends by agreeing with what I've done.

A.F. How do you provoke it?

J.C. By re-shuffling. I've been using that method ever since *Le Sang d'un Poète*, when I shifted and reversed the order of the music in every single sequence. Not only did the contrast heighten the relief of the images, but I even

found at times that that 'displaced' music ad-
hered too closely to the gestures, and seemed to
have been written on purpose. For *La Belle et la
Bête* Georges Auric wrote his score to match
the images, which made it almost impossible
for me to break a single rhythm without being
discourteous to the composer. The music was so
beautiful that I felt that Auric, who is against
explanatory music, had deliberately used the
method of contrasts, slow choruses fastened on
quick action, and so on. But on the other hand
when with *Orphée* I picked up, after twenty
years' interval, the thread of *Le Sang d'un Poète*
in which I had played the same theme with one
finger as it were (I know I'm repeating myself
but I can't help that), I took the most irreverent
liberties with the composer. I recorded Auric's
music without the images (to a chronometer)
and for example put the scherzo he had composed for the comic home-coming scene into
the chase through the deserted house. Or, even
better, I recorded Eurydice's lament, by Gluck,
meaning to use it only for the wireless in the
cottage. But when I cut into Auric's music at the
first shot of Heurtebise's entrance, I noticed that
the first and the last note of Gluck's music fitted
exactly with the first and last images of the
scene, and I shamelessly took advantage of that
little miracle. Miracles of that kind are fairly
common with people who calculate only by

instinct. The same thing happened, for example, in *Les Enfants Terribles*, where I found that Bach's *andante* coincided faultlessly with the scene of Paul in the nocturnal hall, from the moment he comes in up to the moment when he lies down.

Another disrespectful liberty I took: I made a record of the drums of Katherine Dunham's band, and superimposed it on the final orchestra of *Orphée*, going as far as occasionally cutting out some of the orchestral music and leaving only the drums. I am telling you this because I heard Auric say on the radio that he approved of what I'd done, and recognized that these director's cuts gave added force and presence to his music.

A.F. As *La Belle et la Bête* was the first film you made entirely by yourself, I suppose you took René Clément as an assistant to reassure you on the technical side? Were you afraid that some details might escape you?

J.C. This might have been the reason why I originally chose Clément. But gradually we both noticed that his whole training and approach clashed with all my methods. He was very nice and pretended that I was teaching him a new profession, but in fact I found support in his methods, for my efforts to break with tradition helped me to find new ones. Our collaboration was delightful. He was then editing his *Bataille du Rail* and we worked in concert on both those films, so opposite to one another. Not that I played the slightest part in *Bataille du Rail*, but a fresh eye enabled me to make a few suggestions, and Clément's eye, accustomed to the rhythm of his own film, contributed to mine in exchange.

The only tragic part of the making of *La Belle et la Bête* was Jean Marais's terrible make-up which used to take five hours and from which he emerged as though after a surgical operation. Laurence Olivier said to me one day that he would never have had the strength to undergo such torture. I maintain that it took both Marais's passion for his profession and his love for his dog to have persisted with such fortitude to pass from the human race into the animal one. What was in fact due to the genius of an actor was ascribed by the critics to the perfection of a mask. But there was no mask, and to live the part of the Beast, Marais in his dressing-room went through the terrible phases of Dr. Jekyll's transformation into Mr Hyde.

As to Mademoiselle Josette Day's performance in the part of *la Belle*, it had a peculiarity that very few people noticed. She has been a dancer. Now it is very dangerous to use slow motion for a person who is running. Every fault of movement is revealed. This is why a race horse or a boxing match can be so beautiful in slow motion, and why a crowd is so ridiculous.

All these are only small points, but if I've dwelt on them at some length it is because I thought it would be useful to explain to attentive readers the thousand and one pitfalls of a job which seems so simple to the public. At every step we find a new one gaping at our feet. Therefore our feet have to be very nimble. And this is where the wonderful French worker saves the game. Nothing can be more sensitive than the old worn-out shoes of those silent men shuffling about among a kind of work that might have been expected to surprise them but which detail by detail they come to know so well.

Ruy Blas: Jean Marais in the title role. (Courtesy National Film Archive of the British Film Institute)

Ruy Blas: Danielle Darrieux as the Queen. (Courtesy National Film Archive of the British Film Institute)

A.F. Shall we now speak about the film that followed *La Belle et la Bête—Ruy Blas?*

J.C. With *Ruy Blas*, the idea was to make a Western, a cloak and dagger film. My substance was not involved in that film, for it corresponded rather to a game than to an inner necessity. That's why I entrusted the making of it to a director whom I only assisted as it were, and whose rhythm I couldn't alter. A film, whatever it might be, is always its director's portrait. And *Ruy Blas*, badly misunderstood by the famous élite and very popular with the masses, reflected Pierre Billon's mischievous charm.

Again, both he and I were filled with wonder at the subtlety and understanding of the studio craftsmen. We set the plasterers, for instance, a well-nigh impossible task: to sculpt a false Spain without ever losing sight of her romanticism. They hunted among a mass of queer documents which were to Spain what Viollet-le-Duc was to

77

the Middle Ages. Thanks to them and to Wak-hevitch, I was able at last to give body to one of my dreams: to suspend constructions in the void without resorting to backdrops. We had a Spanish hulk outlined against velvet as black as the Indian ink of Victor Hugo's drawings.

A.F. I would like to discuss the films in which you did 'involve your substance': *L'Aigle à Deux Têtes*, *Les Parents Terribles*, and, lastly, *Orphée*. And can I put *Les Enfants Terribles* on the same list?

J.C. *Les Enfants Terribles* was an adventure of a special kind. Up till then, I had declined all the offers to film the story, but I accepted Melville's because his free-lance style seemed well suited for communicating to the film that improvised '16-mm.' air I alluded to earlier on. Besides, our lack of capital and stars implied using real settings. We shot in Melville's flat, an awful place which made his wife quite miserable, and which he specially rented with that venture in view. We shot in railway carriages. We shot in the incredible lobby of the *Petit Journal* whose monumental hideousness surpasses anything one might invent on purpose. We shot at the '*Laurent*' in the Avenue Gabriel, and even, when Melville was ill, I shot a summer beach scene in Montmorency under snow.

The only studio facilities we had recourse to

(for the room) were those of the Théâtre Pigalle whose utterly unworkable machinery, for once, rendered us enormous service. For instead of trying to hoist up the camera with cranes that don't exist in France, we lowered the mobile stage down to the cellars. The film was torn to shreds by the critics, but for my part I cannot praise it enough. I know I wouldn't be able to re-read my book without seeing it from the angle of that film, and without lending to my heroes the faces of Nicole Stéphane and Edouard Dermit. The only reservation I have to make is about the pupil, Dargelos. Melville insisted on giving both that part and that of Agathe to the same girl. But Dargelos as a character is extremely virile, endowed with a prestige that can only belong to a boy proud of his male prerogatives, so that no amount of talent on the part of an actress could make the character plausible.

For the rest, I repeat, I bow and maintain that one day that film will be classed among the best. I'm almost forgetting Johann Sebastian Bach, whose funereal joyousness accords sublimely with the plot. Shall I tell you a nice story? After the film came out, if anybody went to a gramophone shop to ask for a record of that concerto for four pianos, the shop assistant said: 'You mean the music of *Les Enfants Terribles*?' This reminds me of another very funny story. I was staying in Toulon with George Davis, a young American who is now running in New York several periodicals with colossal sales. At that time the Toulon cinemas were showing a film with the actor Bach, entitled *En Bordée* .* One day Davis, absentminded as usual, entered a music shop and asked if they had any Bach. '*En Bordée?*' asked the girl. 'No,' Davis gravely replied, '*en fugues.*'

A.F. *Les Enfants Terribles* leads us to *Les Parents Terribles.*

J.C. Although this was made earlier, it's the right order. I must admit that cinematically speaking *Les Parents Terribles* is my biggest achievement. In that film, as Barrès would say, I looped the loop. I had set out to do three things: firstly, record the acting of an incomparable cast; secondly, walk among them and look them straight in the face, instead of contemplating them at a distance on the stage; thirdly, peep through the key-hole and catch my wild beasts unawares with my tele-lens. I may be wrong, but it seems to me that instead of expanding the play, as I did with *L'Aigle à Deux Têtes* (which was made earlier but of which I'll speak later), I drew it in, I condensed it, and cut out innumerable 'traditions', that is, the 'Ah's' and 'Oh's', the mannerisms inevitable in

* On the spree. (Transl.)

the theatre where actors settle down in their parts and wear them out of shape like clothes.

On the screen the play regained the strength of writing, and that blackness of ink that is watered down by the footlights. While roaming through the rooms, I managed to preserve the closed atmosphere of the play. I showed the thunder-laden corridors which had haunted my childhood, and which are the streets of families that never go out.

I'd like to speak about each one of the five actors, who are like Andersen's winds raging in the cave. I feel that the very perfection of their acting made it invisible, restraining the praise that was given them and the gratitude that is mine. Madame de Bray burst without any preparation into a new profession that seemed quite the opposite of her usual disorder. The incredible thing was that she sacrificed nothing to it, and a few minutes were sufficient to make her understand that one can't move on the studio floor otherwise than by following chalk marks and strips of wood. I can truly say that I put a lioness in a cage and that as a result her electricity began to crackle even more intensely. Similar difficulties did not arise with Madame Dorziat, whose skill in a storm is unequalled. I asked Marcel André to break with the bad habit of *far niente* prevailing in the cinematographic school, and not to moderate his gestures; if necessary, not to hesitate to obstruct the camera with his hands. As for Mademoiselle Josette Day, whose beauty handicaps her with the judges, she was a model of modesty and reserve. She was exactly like a bird among hunters. If I've kept Jean Marais to the last, it is because his acting eludes analysis. It was prodigious—all the more so as he was no longer of the age he had been when he created the part in the play, and had to *act* that which he had previously performed instinctively, thus trebling the effects by a mixture of fire and style.

A.F. I was surprised, hearing you speak of *Les Parents Terribles*, to find in you the same preoccupations as when you spoke about *La Belle et la Bête*. You sound as though you had followed the same line without a break, whereas for us there seems to be a break and a deliberate change of style.

J.C. In the first place *Les Parents Terribles* is not a realistic film, for I have never known a family that lives like that. It is the most imaginary painting you can conceive. I made up that family from top to toe because it happened to appeal to me, at the time, to make a tragicomic mixture and to involve my characters by means of a vaudeville plot in situations which Roger Lannes has compared to a scramble in a

Les Parents Terribles: Marcel André and Yvonne de Bray as the parents. (Courtesy National Film Archive of the British Film Institute)

Les Parents Terribles: Jean Marais as the son. (Courtesy
National Film Archive of the British Film Institute)

house on fire, when people crush each other at the door. The notion of realism seems to awaken in our judges' minds only at the sight of scenes of streets and working-class houses. Thus they have christened 'neo-realistic' the films in which our Italian comrades deploy a power of imagination worthy of Arab storytellers. Just as Haroun al Raschid put on a disguise in order to overhear his people's secrets, so they disguise themselves as film-cameras to slip into the lodgings of the poor, climb up and down the stairs, walk along the pavements, in short, register the minutest details of adventures which are as eccentric and unreal as the adventures in a dream. This is one of the reasons why when I made a film of *Les Parents Terribles* I made a point of not losing its theatrical flavour even though adopting a filmic one. As I have said before, what I tried to do was merely to gather in, condense, compress, keeping clear of that realism in which one tends to clothe a film whenever it doesn't wear costume. For me, and I say this without the slightest hint at a paradox, *La Belle et la Bête*, *L'Aigle à Deux Têtes* and *Orphée* are quite as realistic as *Les Parents Terribles*, for the excellent reason that all films are realistic in that they *show* things instead of suggesting them in words. What is seen is seen. Thereby it becomes *true*, in the sense in which Goethe uses the word.

A.F. What is that Goethian *truth?*

J.C. It is a truth that will force me to contradict myself, as is apt to happen in conversations like the one we're having now. Goethe opposes the 'truth' by which the artist expresses himself and even his lies, to the 'reality' which can produce no more than a flat copy of the model. Do you remember the anecdote where he shows Eckermann a Rubens engraving and asks him if he understands why he finds it so beautiful? Eckermann (as was only to be expected) replies that he does not, and Goethe (as was to be expected) seizes the opportunity to demonstrate that the shadow of the sheep which should have been on their left is on their right, by which subterfuge, Goethe says, the artist has dominated nature and proved himself. So I shouldn't have spoken to you of 'realism'. I should have said 'truthism'. In the sense that we endeavour to approach not *the* truth which objectively doesn't exist, but *a* truth which is subjectively ours.

A.F. Bearing this in mind, what is the place one ought to give productions such as *The Bicycle Thieves*, *Paisà*, *Sunday in August* and the like, which probably appear in the spectators' eyes as being the very opposite of your own work?

J.C. The most important thing to say in this connection is something which I've already mentioned when I spoke of Buñuel and which very few people are aware of, namely that in every given epoch men who create on a certain level, that is, invent, are connected, know and esteem each other, whilst their respective partisans pit them against each other. Every time Orson Welles, Rossellini, de Sica, or Emmer, not to mention Clouzot, Bresson and other front-rank men, bring out a new film, they show it to me, just as I show them my films before anybody else has had a chance to interfere. But as we don't proclaim our family affairs from the house-tops, the uninformed imagine that we're very far apart, and don't see the affinities of style behind the visible diversity. This brings me back to what Buñuel once said: it's this style which is *style*, that in the long run cancels out the differences of the present day and eventually leads to a confusion between works of art which seemed antagonistic to each other when they came out.

Such a confusion is impossible where there is absence of style, and only a vague family resemblance, due to the artist's efforts to keep abreast of his time and take advantage of the latest left-wing fashion. Whilst the style I am speaking of can only spring from the intense urge of a human mind to express itself down to its innermost depths, in any form whatsoever.

A.F. How do you tell the difference between true kinship and vague family resemblance?

J.C. I recognize it at first sight. I could say it's an inner voice, but that would be inaccurate. I can tell it by the malaise, the inopportuneness, the lameness, in a word, the discomfort that emanates from all brotherly works. With the others everything flows too fast and walks too straight. That is the reason of their immediate success. They never worry anybody, they don't disturb anyone's comfort, don't provoke any malaise, and all this leads our judges to imagine that they are contemplating an expression of relief, a completion of preliminary sketches. The film *Les Enfants Terribles*, on the other hand, is a typical instance of the discomfort I have in mind.

The festival of the *films maudits* in Biarritz, for which, alas, we didn't have enough exhibits, was in intention an excellent enterprise. Our aim was to restore into circulation the gold that had been driven down into the cellars by paper currency; to try to give a new start to a few masterpieces which when they first came out alienated the public by their atmosphere of discomfort. But I repeat and I'll never cease repeating—can such grave problems find any solution in the fleeting world of films? Can we hope that technical progress won't make it impracticable to exhibit films that we proudly hold to be the great classics of the screen?

A.F. Let's speak about these classics. What are your favourites?

J.C. The best films have been made by the Russians. Last night I saw *Sebastopol* again, which is, together with Eisenstein's films and the extraordinary *Storm over Asia*, the type of narrative in which montage provides the visual equivalent of the writing style of a Tolstoy. Imagine what a genius it would take to *describe* in words what a film made in that way can *show*.

The film was dubbed (which I don't reject), and well dubbed. The powerful performance of the leading actor was not affected in the least. A Dostoievski style translated into visual terms is not so easy to imagine. All its effectiveness is internal.

A.F. We musn't forget, now that you've spoken of *Les Parents Terribles*, that between that film and *La Belle et la Bête* you made *L'Aigle à Deux Têtes*, which seems to me to be a bridge between the fantastic and the lyrically human.

J.C. Nothing is more difficult to disentangle than the affair of *L'Aigle à Deux Têtes*, both play and film. The play was a repudiation of the theatre of words and of the theatre of stage-production. I brought the public back quite bluntly to the *theatre of action*—action that saves the audience from the boredom which most of them take for seriousness. They had been going to school. It was high time to get them out of it. You may say that pupils adore the hubbub of the end of the school day; but we must remember that, at the school I'm speaking of, each pupil watched the others out of the corner of his eye and didn't want to seem a dunce. That school therefore threatened to go on for ever, to become petrified in its habits and regard any kind of recreation as pleasure unworthy of its dignity. Recently we saw glaring evidence of that when Jean Louis Barrault revived *Le Bossu*. The spectators were completely taken in and felt ashamed of themselves only upon awakening, that is to say in the cloakroom. Another thing. The failure of my film with the judges was largely due to the fact that having previously decried my play they could now begin praising it in order to condemn the film. I admit that the film version of *L'Aigle à Deux Têtes* contains some parentheses and excursions which lead the work away from its centre (an error I didn't commit in *Les Parents Terribles*, where in filming the play I wound it even tighter around its centre). It is none the less true that these mistakes, that one forgives in other films which sometimes wander off so far that one loses sight of the centre altogether, should not have prevented my judges from taking some notice of sequences such as the one in the Queen's room, where I employed a method I had learned during my walks around the cat-walks in the flies of the Hébertot theatre. From there I had a chance to catch some glimpses of my play from another angle than the dead angle of the stalls. I realized the reason why the worst seats are the best. The expensive seats leave the spectators out in the cold; whereas the cheap seats do to some extent the job of the film camera, giving the audience some very curious viewpoints, as though they were indiscreetly peeping through portholes, key-holes or trap-doors into cellars. I insist on the word 'indiscreet'. The camera is the most indiscreet and the most immodest eye in the world. So much so that some actors feel embarrassed, as I observed with Madame Feuillère, for instance, when in the theatre she noticed that the spectators, who had grown accustomed to close-ups, fabricated them for themselves with opera-glasses. We are often driven to the mistake of enlarging space or time by our backers who imagine that exterior shots give a breath of fresh air and facilitate that stupid 'evasion' for which one ought to substitute *invasion*, collective hypnosis of a public that one does not awaken and that one forces finally to look deep into itself.

A.F. These evasions are not entirely indefensible, however, for I myself, having written about Elizabeth of Austria, of whom one can't help thinking when one sees your Queen, and having no idea where you shot your exteriors, sensed the truthfulness of the *décor* and costumes, which seemed familiar to me, as anyone who is sufficiently fascinated by a subject to write about it tends to regard it as his private property.

J.C. Our mistake, Bérard's and mine, was to be too truthful, without any historical touch. People nowadays don't know anything about queens. They have a conventional idea about them, whereas the only thing that matters is the truth. To cite just one instance, we have often been criticised in the press for the Queen's iron bedstead, so unlike the elaborate affair of *Love Parade*. But the fact is that that bed was the one young Queen Victoria had slept in. No doubt the flashy ornaments of *Love Parade* were right, for they succeeded in dazzling many people, and the real bed was wrong because it was moving only for a few. But I'd better stop here. Otherwise we'll never cease going round and round in the circle of the eternal problem of art for the crowds.

L'Aigle à Deux Têtes: Jean Marais as the young revolution-
ary. (Courtesy National Film Archive of the British Film
Institute)

L'Aigle à Deux Têtes: Edwige Feuillère as the Queen. (Courtesy National Film Archive of the British Film Institute)

L'Aigle à Deux Têtes: Feuillère and Marais. (Courtesy
National Film Archive of the British Film Institute)

L'Aigle à Deux Têtes: the Queen with her companion (Sylvia Monfort) and an officer. (Courtesy National Film Archive of the British Film Institute)

A.F. And yet didn't *L'Aigle à Deux Têtes,* which seemed designed to satisfy the most delicate taste, turn out to be first and foremost extremely popular with mass audiences?

J.C. This is because mass audiences don't bother about details. All they want is to follow the story that's being told to them, and they believe in it to the extent to which its pictures are imposed upon them. But the élite shies and kicks against any compulsion to see and hear as we do. It hasn't learnt the sleep that delivers us to a dream. It pinches itself in order to keep awake. 'They're forcing me to look at this queen in this way when I imagine her in another? I will resist.' The great civilizations are those where the acutest and most wide-awake élites don't struggle against the spell of Theatre and Music, and are willing to go to sleep.

A.F. You keep coming back to the lack of understanding on the part of the élite. But what compels you to go and put your head into the lion's mouth, at first nights and gala performances, which you attend only when a work of yours is produced?

J.C. I hold these gala nights in such abomination that I left Paris for Nice on the eve of the ballet *Phèdre* at the Opéra. As to films, that's a different story. We are surrounded by a world fettered by customs which we succeed in overcoming during the shooting of the film, but which we haven't enough strength to vanquish afterwards. Besides, the world, while it reluctantly agrees to follow us upon a path that it considers wrong, does not agree to break with habits that enable it to debunk the result of our efforts, of which it disapproves but which may perhaps do it credit. This ceremonial legalizes, as it were; it helps and surrounds what it regards as dangerous by municipal guards with drawn swords. It knows in advance that that first audience will be cold, elegant and polite. And after that it leaves it to very scant publicity to advertise the work it holds in such contempt as being the most impressive and wonderful show in the world. Our chances in the face of such obstructions are very slight. We can count only on the film's travels, when space will play the role of time and allow the film to be viewed from a proper distance, impossible to achieve at home.

A.F. I believe that the film *L'Aigle à Deux Têtes* was first performed in England. Were you present? And what was your impression in a country where royalty still exists?

J.C. I think, for I don't know English well enough to be quite certain, that Ronald Duncan had to curb his adaptation of the play to some definite exigencies, which probably accounted for its success. But the film must have scandalized an audience composed of princes and ambassadors. I attended the performance with the Duchess of Kent, whose feeling of discomfort which, as she admitted to me, came from a striking coincidence with the tragedies of her own family, must have been contagious and chilling for the whole audience. That reserve, which I sensed through every pore of my skin, affected me much more than enthusiasm would have done. It couldn't be directed against me personally, as I knew from the success in England of *Orphée* and *La Belle et la Bête*. Searching a little deeper, however, I can perhaps find another reason for that reserve in the fact that Bérard and I had avoided the aestheticism that still appeals to many people in England. I dare say we were too true for some and not true enough for others. Some countries were attracted to the film but hesitated to exhibit it to the public, namely those countries which consider themselves to be the custodians of the prestige of an Empress whose personality, however, inspired us only in a general way, without our using any exact historical facts. All we took from her was a certain superficial air, to which, however, it would have been difficult to avoid referring, as that Princess was the only one who displayed in real life the opulence that a few great actresses had exhibited on the stage.

There is some bric-à-brac of Sarah Bernhardt's in the gymnasium in which I placed the only incident that was factually true (which was precisely the one the public held to be inaccurate), when the Minister of Police is received by his Queen dressed in a long gown and swinging on a trapeze.

It was no doubt obedience to theatrical protocol that dictated to us that single instance of picturesqueness which Bérard and I had so consistently avoided everywhere else. Which made our critics complain that *La Belle et la Bête* lacked flourish, and that the suburban ruins of *Orphée* ought to have been a Dante circle.

Every time one slips into the picturesque, the spectators grab hold of it as though it were a lifebelt in a shipwreck. They have no eyes for anything else. Whenever people begin speaking about *Orphée* and don't know how to get out of it, they swoop down like so many flies on the one slip into picturesqueness that I was guilty of in that film: the negatives on the road. Likewise in *La Belle et la Bête* they pounce upon the sheet scene. Speaking about such flies settling on the dance of the bread-rolls in *The Gold Rush*, Chaplin confessed to me that they had made him long to cut it out. It's rather like somebody saying, after attending a performance of Goethe's *Faust*, 'I liked the red of Mephistopheles's cap.' Nobody ever blames Giraudoux or René Clair for the traits that are characteristic of them. But every time one sees a statue or a candelabra in a film of mine (and in *La Belle et la Bête* I did no more than follow the story, in which there is such a profusion of statues and candelabras that I left out the episode of the sisters being changed into statues) I'm caned for it. People complain about my bric-à-brac. 'There isn't a single gaiter-button missing,' a critic said about *Les Enfants Terribles*. I should hope not! I made it. Why should there be any gaiter-buttons missing? It was my job to see that it should be complete down to the last button.

A.F. Since we are back again on the chapter of critics, which was the criticism regarding any of your films that struck you as the most unfair?

J.C. François Chalais's about *Les Enfants Terribles*, when he declared that I was 'gaily killing off my children'. I retorted that he was gaily killing off my young actors, which was much more serious, for my children existed only in my dreams whereas my actors were children in real life. François Chalais is a friend and I don't bear any grudge against him. I am convinced that if films could be presented without the rush and chaos imposed by the conditions prevailing in the big cities of the world, the critics would view them with different eyes and would familiarize themselves with them, as do those who follow their making minute by minute. An example: *Le Château de Verre*, a film by René Clément based on a story by Vicki Baum. In the film, the plot is simplified in the extreme. It is the story of a young man incapable of love and of his mistress who pretends she's leaving him completely free, but gets extremely worried about a girl from Berne. Will he fall in love with her? The girl from Berne gets killed in an air crash. Monsieur Jean Fayard declared that he didn't understand what it was all about, which means that he confessed to his incapacity to follow a simple plot. At the end of the film there's a very good touch: the girl from Berne says to her lover that people can control time as they please, and jokingly puts the hands of her watch forward. They happen to hit on the hour when she will die. Thereupon the director cuts to a sequence where the girl's husband is told on the telephone that his wife has just died on her way to Paris. Then we come back to the hands of the watch, and everything goes on in the right order. The young woman misses her train, boards an aeroplane and leaves. We know that she will die. Monsieur Jean Fayard interprets the telephone scene with her husband as a 'premonitory dream'. Such a mistake, which is utterly unforgivable, misled a multitude of readers.

A.F. I am surprised to see how sensitive you are to some criticisms and how indifferent to others.

J.C. I'm very sensitive about inaccuracy of any sort. When I tell people something, they always think I've made it up, and yet I never tell them anything other than what I've seen or heard. I do my best to report it as precisely as possible. I don't agree with journalists who think that an accurate report is sure to bore the readers, and who disfigure facts to please them. It's a distorted image of the Fable. To the 'truer than truth', which is our kind of fable, they oppose the 'falser than falsehood'.

A.F. I would be interested to hear how you succeed in reconciling the two major exigencies that haunt you and seem to contradict each other: your work is so rich and at the same time condensed; it 'spares its breath'; and yet you demand immediate accuracy on the part of your critics.

J.C. It is quite simple. We are all made of mud, and gravity compels us to fall back into it very quickly. There are moments when we see ourselves clearly, and there are moments when we should like other people to see us clearly. It is this contrast that creates the interplay between presence and solitude, between our plunges into the human sea where we catch cold, and the fireside chair in the country. I am aware that all I'm saying to you now may be confusing for the reader. But as my only training has been endeavouring to keep my balance at every given moment, I am incapable of skipping over a single inch of the way. Contradictions are the fabric we're made of, and although I know what an advantage it is for an artist to simplify his line, to make it thicker and easier to see, I don't do it, perhaps through laziness, or perhaps in obedience to a moral rule which I have set myself and which I call honesty.

A.F. Now we come to *Orphée*, an extremely important film which winds up all your searchings, and sums up twenty years of your work in a medium which, because it is immediate, is dangerous. A film in which more forcibly than ever you have opposed poetry to the 'poetic', and in which those of us who knew *Le Sang d'un Poète* have felt at home. Will you tell me in detail how you made that film? And whether the position you had gained through your other films (a position the continuity of which you have just proved to me) has made it easier for you to carry out a project that would have been beyond the reach of a newcomer?

J.C. A book never ensures the success of another book. And a film, unless it is the copy of a previous one, encounters the same difficulties as those that hamper a newcomer. My first interview with the high-ranking officials of the Crédit National gave me good proof of that. As they began quibbling over my script, I cut them short and suggested that they might trust me, seeing that I had been very prompt in refunding all the credits they had granted me in the past. 'But how can you say we don't trust you?' these gentlemen said. 'Why, if an unknown young man submitted such a script to us we'd throw him out.'

This terrible sentence seems to sum up the sole advantage of having a reputation such as mine. For the rest, I had to proceed exactly as though I were a newcomer: I founded a small company, scrounged around for every penny, and cut down on the costing; and in the end I managed to scrape through only thanks to my cast who generously agreed to share the risks and wait for payment out of my problematic takings. There can be no doubt that if I had accepted the innumerable and absurd offers I had from various companies, I'd now be a rich man—rich 'under the counter'. But my conception of the cinematograph *versus* cinema condemns me to an unceasing struggle. On only one occasion, in my desire to cover the expenses in excess of costing which I had undertaken to pay off out of my own pocket, did I agree to cook up a story for some Mexican producers— with the result that they went off and shot quite another story (keeping my name on the credit titles), without Madame Maria Félix, who was

Orphée: the grim motorcyclists. (Courtesy National Film Archive of the British Film Institute)

Orphée: Maria Casarès as the Princess. (Courtesy National Film Archive of the British Film Institute)

Orphée: Heurtebise and Eurydice (Marie Dea) before the judges of the other world. (Courtesy Herman G. Weinberg)

playing a part in the film, or any other members of the unit knowing anything about it. This is an example of the kind of trap a film-maker constantly finds gaping at his feet. And this is why I refuse to call myself a film-maker; and also why the money-grubbers were flabbergasted by the success of *Orphée*.

A.F. Why, after all your explorations in various directions, did you come back to the Orpheus myth, which had already inspired a play where you expressed yourself with complete freedom? Why did you deem it necessary to treat the same subject cinematically? And being one of those who saw *Orphée* in the Pitoeff production, I'd also like to know the reasons that determined the differences and the similarities between your play and the film?

J.C. My moral gait is that of a lame man, with one foot in life and the other in death. Therefore I am quite naturally drawn to a myth in which life and death meet face to face. Moreover, and I'll speak to you at length about that later on, I realized that a film would serve much better to show the incidents on the frontier separating the two worlds. It was a manner of using tricks in the same way as a poet uses ciphers, that is, never allowing them to fall into the visible, i.e. into the inelegant, and making them appear as a reality, or rather as a truth to the spectators. You'll understand that this compelled me to overcome the facility accorded by the cinematograph to fantasy and magic. I had to make magic *direct*, without ever using the laboratory and showing only what I saw myself and wanted others to see.

A.F. What do you mean by *direct* magic?

J.C. I mean a magic which, through an equilibrium between imagination and technique, through an extreme preliminary complexity ends by becoming as simple as would be, for a child who had seen sugar dissolve in water, the miracle that he himself does not dissolve in his bath. This equilibrium demands a close and unremitting understanding between the head cameraman and the director. Nicholas Hayer and myself, after our failure with conjurers and music-hall experts, sought only for means of showing on the screen what we had seen ourselves. This is the method of poets, who collect information but never use it. We had to give up our experiments with mirrors without silvering and with black velvet because they proved unusable in film lighting. I'll add, however, that such failures were useful in that they excited our imagination and set it going, compelling it to solve the problem of trick effects without resorting to any tricks.

A.F. It seems to me that already in *Le Sang d'un Poète*, when you were only a beginner and a dilettante, you invented a classic form of trick effect which has never been improved upon.

J.C. This is because my inventions in *Le Sang d'un Poète* were like children's sayings, which have so much poetic force. I didn't know a thing. I had to learn my trade at any cost, and I believed that I was using what I had learnt in the usual way. As a result, many of my mistakes passed for discoveries. For instance, Charlie Chaplin took it for a discovery of mine when a figure that moved in a medium close shot began his movements all over again in the close-up, instead of ending. But I was simply bad at cutting and had made a mistake. Similarly, the shot of the poet walking through the looking-glass set the whole of America wondering why that shot had none of the rigidity of rails. But I didn't know that such rails existed, and the actor in my film was drawn on a plank fixed on rollers. I did it again, this time deliberately, in *La Belle et la Bête* when Beauty walks along the corridors with flying curtains. Mistakes and chance happenings are often useful. At the end of *Les Parents Terribles*, for instance, when the camera moved away from the subject, the rough ground and the rickety dolly made the retreating image shake and jog about. It occurred to me to keep that bad shot and turn it into a good one. To that initial fault I added the noise of cart wheels, and said the last phrase about gypsies.

A.F. But do you often resort to dolly shots? They seem to me like the film-maker's "old standby."

J.C. Except on very rare occasions, the movement of the camera cancels the movement of the subject. If you follow a racing horse it will run without moving. But if you make it pass again and again in front of a stationary camera fixed successively at different angles, the movement will be seen and intensified tenfold. In *Les Parents Terribles* the camera moved very little, but I changed the angles a great deal. I used the same method in *L'Aigle à Deux Têtes*, in the Queen's bedroom, when Edwige Feuillère paces up and down, moving away and then pouncing upon the silences of Jean Marais. This method, however, finds its final shape only at the montage stage. Montage is style. A director who doesn't edit his own films allows himself to be translated into a foreign tongue. But I've already said that.

A.F. Let's come back to *Orphée*. How did you manage to avoid laboratory tricks, which you call 'picturesque' and which you loathe? How, for example, do your characters walk in and out of mirrors?

J.C. In a different way each time. Our subterfuges were based on the fact that in a film a mirror isn't taken into account, but only the void, or, rather, the frame. We built twin rooms and filled them with twin objects, and if you look carefully enough you can easily notice it, for in the mirror (which doesn't exist) every image is reversed except the little engravings on the wall and the bust on the chest of drawers. I relied entirely on a card-trick speed. Do you realize that it would have been impossible to take some of the shots if we had been facing a proper mirror reflecting the camera and the camera crew? When Maria Casarès opens a three-leafed mirror, it would have been impossible for her to walk out of a two-dimensional surface. She walked out of the second room. A double, dressed like her and back to back to her, walked off in the opposite direction, playing the part of her reflection. The funny thing was that Maria Casarès changed three times during that scene (a black dress, a grey and a white), and that as my finances forbade me to reproduce all three, when Casarès had a black dress on, her reflection wore a grey one. Nobody noticed anything, and I assure you that I myself was duped when I saw the rushes, which shows to what extent a truth fabricated by us can be convincing, owing to the mere fact that it is *seen*. It has all the persuasiveness of a false witness. Another instance: when Marais goes towards the mirror and raises his rubber-gloved hands, a portable camera is placed on the shoulder of a studio-hand wearing a jacket and wet gloves similar to Marais's. Thus I was able to approach facing the false room, from the back of which Marais in person advanced, playing the part of his own reflection. The gloved hands met. I cut, and passed on to another angle. Such an effect requires all the skill of the camera operator and the focus man, for neither the close up nor the medium shot must be blurred. The new American lenses permit that. Ours do not. All rests, as I have said before, upon the skill of craftsmen whose mental agility enables them to catch up with the progress of technique.

In some of the shots I made Nicholas Hayer's task easier by substituting (in the Court scene) the real characters for the fictitious ones. This muddled people, presenting both childish difficulties and truly baffling riddles. You see the reflection of the judges: those are the judges themselves. But what is muddling is that Maria Casarès in the foreground, seen from the back, is the real Maria Casarès.

When Jean Marais and François Périer

appear in the court room, Marais leaps in slow motion through the empty frame in which we saw (in the same shot) one of the motor cyclists playing the part of the reflection of another motor cyclist (they were two brothers). I cut, and take Marais motionless. After that he moves back and his movement draws the camera with him towards Périer in front of a real mirror (quickly substituted in the meantime) from which he seems to have emerged saying the line, '*Nous sommes faits comme des rats*'. I forgot to explain that when Jean Marais jumps, he jumps backwards through an identical frame (since the real judges are supposed to be their reflections in the mirror). The entire mechanism, which oftens remains a riddle even for those who take part in it, falls into place in the projecting room, where the whole unit rushed every evening in order to understand what they had done entirely on trust during the day.

I don't pretend to have invented the method of having the reflection in a mirror acted by another person. I used it as a syntax. You find it in the Delannoy-Sartre film (done with twin sisters). In fact, none of these things is new. They're all the same old dictionary words. Already Méliès used them, and to use different ones would mean to be emphatic, which is as deplorable in the visual language as it is in writing. Besides, even if a film is made without any attempt at tricks, they are still there. They are the secret arsenal of painting and of poetry. A bad film is like a poet without culture, content to tell a story in verse (with nothing of that which makes a poem a poem).

A.F. I hoped, like many other members of the audience, to have spotted a few of the special effects of *Orphée*. Thus in the dunes, after the scene in the chalet, I thought I noticed a cut in the sound, a deliberate silence.

J.C. This would have been impossible. A cut in the sound would make a hole that is not silence. What you *heard* was real silence, and I insist on the word 'heard' because an attentive ear can detect the thousand and one imperceptible sounds of which that silence is composed. There is deliberate silence, yes. But that silence is derived from the locality itself. And it sometimes happens that the locality resists, refusing to be at our beck and call. The ruins of Saint-Cyr, for instance, (which very nearly caused my own, for the night shooting, as I've already mentioned, cost us a fortune in generating equipment) gave me a nasty shock. There were about one hundred and fifty trains passing there every night. The *sous-préfet*, Amade, stood watch in hand announcing the times of the trains and the intervals in the din.

But it was very rare, alas, that a shot could be made to coincide with the railway timetable. This is why in *Orphée* you occasionally hear distant whistles and a kind of hollow factory noise. We tried to dub these passages. But in the projecting room I realized that the whistles and the factory noises gave a background of mystery to the dialogue, and that they should on no account be cut.

A.F. So you made use of accidental noises as though they were a trick? But have you on any other occasion manipulated sound as you manipulate the pictures?

J.C. I'm quite as interested in the use of sound as in the use of images. When we were making *Le Sang d'un Poète*, as the sound film had just appeared, we kept experimenting till we were quite exhausted. We kept building up walls and then demolishing them, trying in vain to obtain the sound of a crash. At last in desperation I hit upon the discovery that the only way to get that sound was to crumple together two newspapers printed on different paper. I used the *Temps* and the *Intransigeant* (one stiffer than the other). In the same film, with the exception of Rachel Berendt's voice, who dubbed for Miss Lee Miller, all the voices are my own, disguised. The chatter in the theatre

109

box consists of various phrases said by me and made to overlap in the mixing.

A.F. And what about *Orphée?*

J.C. In *Orphée*, for the coming and going through the mirror we used the entire range of the actual sound, but without the initial shock. I kept only the prolongation of the waves (to be in fashion, I should say the undulatory prolongation). I told you about the drums. After shooting the scene where Cégeste rises up in front of the Princess in reverse and in slow motion, I took the whole scene twice in close-up, once with the camera trained on Maria Casarès and once on Dermithe. As the Casarès shots didn't come out very well I kept only the Dermithe ones. But as I liked Dermithe's voice better during the Casarès shots, I put the words of the shots we had taken from behind him on to the shots of the close-up of his face, making them coincide with his lip movements. There are so many subterfuges of that kind in *Orphée* that I couldn't enumerate them all now. But since you seem so interested in these secrets of our trade, and since you think that they might interest the reader, I will tell you about the wall of Saint-Cyr at the corner of which Orphée and Heurtebise fly away. It is a directly filmed trick I had used in *Le Sang d'un Poète*, and which I reproduced in a corridor of the Folies Dramatiques. We built a model of the arcades of Saint-Cyr erected in a horizontal position on a large scaffolding half way up to the ceiling. On the floor, photographed backdrops gave the effect of a distant perspective. We were in a tip-bucket suspended from rails in the flies, so that what we saw when we looked through the camera lying flat on our stomachs were the normal arcades.

At the extreme left-hand corner of that vast contraption was a wooden sheet which sloped down almost perpendicularly and ended in a trench filled with straw. An old woman, leaning her back against some railings suspended over the void, with her legs flat against the *décor*, appeared to be sitting in a niche of the arcade and added to the deception. One saw (although, alas, they could be barely distinguished) two children asleep, lying against a plank in front of one of the fake pavements, in such a position that Orphée and Heurtebise could slip between them and the wall. The two actors (Marais and Périer) had to drag themselves towards the slope without allowing their feet to leave the false ground, which was all there was between them and a long fall; or if they did leave it, they did so with a peculiar clumsiness which, once the picture was set upright, assumed the extraordinary ease of movement of a dream. At the

111

end of that journey, Orphée rolled over the edge and fell down the slope. Heurtebise was supposed to follow him. But Jean Marais is a daredevil, whereas François Périer is not accustomed to that kind of sport. I was afraid to put him to such a test. But after four takes with a stand-in, I realized that I would have to impose that sacrifice on him. He agreed readily, and sprained his ankle in the straw. His sole comment was to ask if the shot was all right, and as it was good (or at least I told him it was, so as not to make him roll down again) he declared that the thing was well worth a sprained ankle, which didn't matter tuppence anyway. That is the kind of man he is.

A.F. I don't want to tire you, but all these details are so fascinating that I must try and record as many as I can. Nobody except you is so willing to speak of what happens behind the scenes, which shows to what extent you are free from relying on secrets and surprises for communicating your poetry.

J.C. Well, here are a few more. The mirror into which Orphée dips his hands required about eight hundredweight of mercury. But there is nothing harder to come by than mercury, and nothing less simple to find than a tank big enough and strong enough to hold it. On top of that, it wouldn't have been safe to keep such a treasure in the Studio. So we had to do the shooting in one day, and we wasted a lot of time because it was almost impossible to get the caps off the drums in which the mercury had been delivered, and because the mercury itself was dirty. It had to be polished with chamois leather, like a silver dish. No sooner had one got that soft heavy surface clean than the impurities rose again and floated on top like oil stains. I thought I might be able to do without Jean Marais by putting the gloves on somebody else of his size. But when I tried I saw that hands were like a person, and we would have to have the actor himself. So he was sent for, and we filmed at six in the evening a shot begun at seven in the morning.

A.F. Why, if it so difficult to handle, did you have to have mercury?

J.C. Because mercury shows only the reflection and not the part that has penetrated into the mirror, as water would have done. In mercury the hands disappear and the gesture is accompanied by a kind of shiver, whereas water would have produced ripples and circles of waves. On top of that, mercury has resistance.

A.F. This provides me with an opportunity to ask you about a shot that must have been extremely difficult, namely when Orphée knocks against the mirror immediately after the last motor cyclist has passed through it.

J.C. You guessed right. As there's only one shot, the motor cyclists couldn't have disappeared if there had been glass. Jean Marais knocked against an empty space and simulated the collision. I added the noise afterwards. The glass was put in only for the following shot, when Marais brushes against it and his cheek is flattened by the pressure. The third shot, in reverse, is taken with a real mirror; the fourth (the one after the room, in the deserted countryside), with a mirror buried in the sand, which plays the part of a glass-like puddle.

Another kind of trick effect, akin to a device used by novelists, is the creation of an unknown deserted little town through a combination of several different districts of Paris. For this, the streets had to be empty of people and extracted from their proper surroundings. The car pulls up at the bottom of the Grenelle steps, at the top of which there is a lamp-post of an unusual shape and some chalky blocks of flats, very much like another unusual lamp-post and some chalky houses in the Square Bolivar (in the Buttes Chaumont district) where Marais enters in the following shot. Maria Casarès disappears in a gateway in the street which runs at the top of that sloping square. Marais dashes in after her, to emerge under the arcades of the Place des Vosges. He turns round the corner and walks into Boulogne, at the covered market where the sequence ends. As to Maria Casarès appearing in the market, it was simply done in two shots and doesn't require any special explanations.

But what I'd find more fascinating than dwelling on the kind of things every film-maker knows, or on the thousand funny incidents which inevitably occur when a crowd that must be hidden persists in trying to be seen, would be to speak about Time and Space. Film art is the only art form that allows us to dominate both. It very seldom happens that adjoining rooms are erected on the same floor, or that an interior set corresponds to the exterior set to which it is supposed to lead. And shooting is very rarely done in the right time order. We are free to manipulate as we please a world in which nothing seems to permit man to over-come his limitations. Not only is our situation similar to that of a painter, who endeavours to transpose the three-dimensional world in which he lives into two dimensions, but what's more, in films these two dimensions express more than three, for we overcome time as well, which is also a dimension, and we can therefore say without any fear of ridicule that we operate in the fourth. In *La Belle et la Bête*, Jean Marais and

Michel Auclair walk into the merchant's house (after the archery tournament) in Touraine, and finish the gesture of shutting the door behind them two months later in Paris, having during all the inadmissible lapse of time led their own lives. It is thanks to the magnificent American camera owned by Pathé (there are only two or three of them in existence) that I was able to shoot Orphée and Heurtebise in the ruins of Saint-Cyr. One is walking (Marais), the other standing motionless (Périer). The atmosphere around the one is dead and diffuse, the other is made animate by wind and light. Marais played his part in Saint-Cyr. François Périer played his much later, in the studio on the banks of the Seine. The system of mirrors is well known and in current use. But for a scene of such precision, where the characters speak to each other and aren't content with merely moving across a given locality, it was imperative to use a perfect machine. I ought to have gone even further, and put two Orphées in the picture, one shoulder to shoulder with Heurtebise and the other behind him. 'Why,' he would have asked, 'are there two of us?' and Heurtebise would have said his line, 'Why, always why? Don't keep asking me questions,' and the rest. Unfortunately a film costs too much money to be corrected after it's been made and, besides, by the time these good ideas come to us it is usually roaming the world over. This is just one more instance of victory over our limitations, and of the kind of work that the laymen who come to visit us don't understand. That's why the visitors in a film studio get bored and cannot follow what's going on, for what they see are only some phenomena of punctuation. They never read a complete sentence.

A.F. I would be tempted to generalize, and to extend your description of visitors in a film studio to life in general, in which time is a phenomenon of perspective, and where we wait without understanding what we are part of and who the director is whom we are expected to obey.

J.C. You are quite right. One always comes back to the amusing reply made by Sainte-Beuve (I think), when somebody declared, 'At bottom, all is in all,' and he said: 'And vice versa.'

A.F. The more you speak, the more you enter into details, the more I become aware of the hard work involved in the creation of a film which is designed for public entertainment but at which the public barely looks, speaking at the same time as the actors, commenting on the story or the actresses' dresses throughout the entire performance.

J.C. Speaking of that kind of public, I can quote a *mot* of Aurélien Scholl which might amuse you. Madame Strauss used to talk a lot during the performance at the theatre. One day she invited Scholl to hear *Faust* in her box, and he replied: 'With the greatest pleasure. I've never heard you in *Faust*.'

Our conversation at this point was interrupted by a telephone call for Jean Cocteau announcing that the British Film Academy had just awarded prizes to twelve films, including two French films—*La Beauté du Diable* and *Orphée*.
Cocteau rang off and said to me:
J.C. *Orphée* has already been awarded the international *grand prix* at the Venice Festival, was chosen for the first crossing of the new *Normandie*, and the *Prix des Spectateurs d'Avantgarde*.* (The awards for *La Belle et la Bête* are innumerable). This is quite a lot for a man who never won a prize at school, and whose name always appeared at the end of the list. That telephone ought to please you. It shows that after its long wanderings, and in spite of all I have previously said, it can happen that a film out of the usual run finds appreciative judges.

---

* Since then the film has won another victory in Cannes, at the referendum of mass audiences and cinema managers.

A.F. I know I've bothered you a lot with questions about your technique, but I should like to ask you just one more: seeing that your shooting script is never final, and that you don't follow it but improvise as you go along, what part of the preliminary work do you consider most important, before the film actually goes on the floor?

J.C. The rhythm I follow is only possible in harmony; therefore the most important thing for me is to choose my collaborators with great prudence.

A.F. To what exactly do you apply such prudence?

J.C. I choose my cast, my technicians and all my workers according to their moral value rather than their artistic value. The latter can be taken for granted, for we can hesitate only between people whose qualifications are first-rate. What matters, therefore, is to see that all the elements of the unit compose a harmonious whole and are moved by the same love of their work. As I've already had occasion to tell you, film making is an interplay of cogs which don't know either the machine as a whole or what the finished product is intended to be. The director alone holds in his mind a single line. But for each one collaborating with him, that line is broken up into a thousand little bits.

That moral value that I seek, besides forging a bond between separate elements and making them gravitate towards one centre, endows the actors' eyes with a quality without which a film like *Orphée* would lose all its profound significance. The beauty of the soul, which the film camera records just like any other vibration (for proof of this, see the difference between a building photographed and a building filmed), is more important for me than physical beauty. The beauty of François Périer, although it's never mentioned in illustrated magazines, is in my eyes just as effective as that of Jean Marais, which the same magazines praise to the skies. They are equals in spiritual beauty. And I would never have joined the fate of Maria Casarès with that of Edouard Dermithe if I hadn't been certain that their reserve, their nobility and their inner fire would make concord.

A.F. May I point out to you that all the recipes you give away so generously, all these secrets of your trade, are hardly ever divulged in periodicals or even in private conversations between film people? Isn't it dangerous to lift the curtain on the machinery behind the scenes?

J.C. A work of art should be strong enough to allow the curtain to be lifted. A professional secret is not of much help for someone who lacks the ability to use it. As Picasso once said to me: **'Skill in one's craft can't be learnt.'**

A.F. If this is so, what would you regard as the best kind of film school?

J.C. It shouldn't be a school at all. The pupils should be allowed to watch the fabrication of several films. For this, one would have to demolish the walls that stand in their way and pull down the barbed wire with which film technique is bristling. I well know that the studio floor is soon congested, and there are always too many people around, whilst our work requires peace and silence. But we'd rather put up with a few young students than with a crowd that always manages to slip through the forbidden doors. If a young man expresses the desire to work as an assistant in a film, he's told that he must first have directed three films himself. I must say that I don't understand that enigma, and I can only hope that it will disappear one day.

A.F. Of all these instances of absurd and odious chicanery, which is the one that seems to you the most harmful for young students, and hinders them most in becoming part of a medium of expression which should be theirs by right?

J.C. The worst ambush is laid by the young people themselves, in the fashions they set. Fashion, alas, isn't the exclusive privilege of the world of frivolity. Fashions are rampant among the young, among journalists, among all those who do mental work. These fashions are the worst of the lot, for they claim to oppose all fashion and don't recognize themselves for what they are. Those who follow them reject everything genuinely new, that is, everything that doesn't conform to these unavowed fashions and is consequently rejected and despised as retrogression. Woe betide him who doesn't blow the same trumpet as his entire generation. Woe to the extreme speed of our *voltes*, to our *nuances* not as easy to perceive as simple colours.

Anyone who might care to get to the bottom of the system of taboos set up by our young men would not have to go very far. Its limits are surprisingly narrow. Beyond these limits, nothing counts. There is an extraordinary laziness and stubbornness, and obedience to slogans. Everything is either black or white. A thing admitted is not necessarily a thing known. It is admitted, that's all. The things that aren't admitted don't deserve being studied. That is the theme of the beginning of *Orphée*, in the Café des Poètes (*yes* for Cégeste, *no* for Orphée). Orphée suffers from it and tries to find a breach.

He imagines he finds one in the phrases he hears on the radio in the Rolls Royce. But these phrases are Cégeste's. That trap is significant. I doubt if it has been understood. (Orphée, who began by being out of fashion in the good sense, falls back into a fashion.)

Another tragedy of films is that the young members of the audience expect a story and nothing else. It is a habit they have acquired from reading detective novels and translations of American books. This is why the vocabulary of films is so mediocre. A film is expected to prove something, to convey a *message*. People want that because they don't see that the slightest episode, the smallest word, can prove much more. In *Orphée*, there isn't a single sentence or a single gesture that does not play a part and deserve notice. But how does one take notice? One talks to the girl beside one and eats ice cream. Another thing. What is so bad about a language disfigured by abbreviations, apostrophes, slang and so forth, is that it leads to confused thinking unable to perceive balance or proportions. Modern architecture is also an example of that.

It shows that minds and souls are living without a syntax, that is to say, without a moral system. This moral system has nothing to do with morality proper, and should be built up by each one of us as an inner style, without which no outer style is possible.

There are a good many more reasons for the

distance that separates our works from our audiences. Probably our spiritual light is a result of disintegration, just as the sun and everything that burns. Of *our* disintegration. And also, probably, our light, like that of stars, takes a long time to reach other minds, so that sometimes it reaches them in a phantom state, as is the case with stars we see long after they have vanished. What can be seen at once is not the light of the spirit. It is the flare of straw, bonfires and fireworks. I will add that contemporaries, without knowing it, live in different epochs—which doesn't make things any easier.

A.F. I'd like to come back to the fashions you have spoken of. Are they merely fashions of artistic appreciation, or do you find some traces of them in the work itself, among the young people who assist you?

J.C. Naturally. Just as some things count and some don't, the young film-makers have their own *ukases*.

A.F. Where do these *ukases* come from?

J.C. From school. Even though these very youngsters should break away from school and laugh at the *ukases* they are taught. I am sixty-one and am constantly involved in disputes over these *ukases*.

A.F. Such as?

J.C. Not to look into the camera. (Wrong; doesn't matter in the least). Direction of the gaze. (Wrong; doesn't matter). When you go out at one side of the picture you must come in on the other side. (Wrong; doesn't matter). The 180 degrees. The 180 degrees is an inviolable taboo. Whenever I decide to have one, all the faces around me lengthen. The assistant and the assistant-trainee announce that they decline all responsibility. In the scene where the Rolls-Royce carrying Orphée's body pulls up on the road, three 180 degrees in succession put all my young colleagues' backs up. But in all fairness I must say that when the editing was done they recognized that I had been right and that the effectiveness of the images was entirely due to that heresy.

The first shot: The Rolls Royce pulls up, flanked by the motor cyclists. Second shot (180 degrees): one of the motor cyclists, taken from the opposite angle, comes up to the door of the car and questions Heurtebise. Third shot (180 degrees): the camera, from the first angle, shows Orphée lying stretched out on the car cushions. Fourth shot (180 degrees): a close-up, again opposite to the last, shows the dead face of Orphée hanging down from the seat. The Rolls Royce moves away, and the camera, passing from the face to the whole scene, shows the car and the motor cyclists driving away.

Such scandals are the grammar of all thoroughbred directors. The school persists in banishing them. The young, although they are excited by Orson Welles, Ford or the Italians, haven't the courage to disobey. Whereas what one should do is give them a portable camera and forbid them to observe any rules except those they invent for themselves as they go. Let them write without being afraid of making spelling mistakes. Not that I specially recommend mistakes in spelling, but anything is better than the academism that hides behind the false novelty of cinematographic teaching.

A.F. *A propos* of academism, what can you say about the symbol-mania, the cluttering up of a film with symbols, against which you have so often warned your colleagues? Doesn't the subject of *Orphée* play into their hands?

J.C. The gratuitous act of which Gide spoke is what the public is least prepared to accept. It wants a meaning for everything. Especially for things whose beauty consists in not having any. People symbolize through passion for logic. For lack of any direct meaning, they make up indirect ones, and reassure themselves by using symbols. Thus with *Orphée*, in which I avoided symbolism and organized a logic of illogicality, they can't refrain from saying that Maria

126

Casarès represents Death, that Heurtebise and the motor cyclists are the Angels of Death, that the ruined suburb is part of Hell, and that the judges are the Judges of the Supreme Tribunal. All of which I deliberately avoided. One Sunday evening I turned on the wireless and heard somebody telling the story of *Orphée*. I caught the sentence: 'Orphée and Heurtebise descend among the subterranean cathedrals of Hell.' What can I do about it? It takes centuries for a work of art to be decanted, to reveal its true nature. Alas! As I have said a thousand times, a film will cease to exist long before justice is done to it. We must be philosophical and patiently endure the innumerable misinterpretations that make it possible for a few lucid minds to see our work and fraternize with us.

A.F. I agree that the symbol-mania is quite absurd. But will you say a little more about your 'logical illogicality' and tell me how you, personally, look upon your heroes?

J.C. All this is said in the film. The locale is 'made of human memories and of the ruins of human habits'. It doesn't encroach on any dogma. It is the No Man's Land between life and death. The moments of coma, as it were. Heurtebise is a dead young man in the service of one of the innumerable employees of Death.

'Orphée: You are all-powerful.

'The Princess: In your eyes. But where I come from we have innumerable figures of death. Young girls, old women, all of us receiving orders.

'Orphée: What if you disobeyed these orders? They couldn't kill you. You are the one who kills.

'The Princess: What they can do is worse.

'Orphée: Where do these orders come from?

'The Princess: They are transmitted by so many sentinels that they are the tom-tom of your African tribes, the echo of your mountains, the wind in the leaves of your forests.

'Orphée: I will go to the one who gives these orders.

'The Princess: My poor love . . . He lives nowhere. Some believe that he thinks about us, others that he thinks us. Others again, that he is sleeping and that we are his dream . . . his bad dream.'

Isn't this clear enough? These characters are as far removed from the Unknown as we are, or nearly. It follows that the motor cyclists of *Orphée* don't know any more about It than our motor-cycle police know about ministerial decisions. The actions of the Princess, which actuate the drama, are taken by her of her own accord and represent free will. A thing must be. It *is*, for what happens to us little by little constitutes in reality one single whole. The entire mystery of free will resides in this, that it seems that the thing that is *need not be*, as is illustrated by the amazing words of Christ: 'Abba, Father, all things are possible unto Thee: take away this cup from me.' Which implies that the whole of time, which we are able to perceive only in perspective, is composed of unthinkable volumes and of a mass of conjoint possibilities. Christ seeks to avert the inevitable. Likewise, the Princess dares to substitute herself for destiny, to decide that a thing *may be*, instead of being, and plays the part of a spy in love with the man she was appointed to watch and whom she saves by losing herself. What is the nature of her loss? What is the punishment to which she exposes herself? This is beyond me, and doesn't concern me any more than do the rites of the beehive or of the ants' nest, those funeral rites whose mystery no entomologist has ever solved. It was essential that some data be missing in my logic, opening breaches into the inaccessible world which it is man's honour to conceive.

A.F. This is complex and clear. And what you have just said so plainly I felt, looking at your film. One would wish that all its spectators would agree to plunge into these depths. Unfortunately, the notion of 'comfort' of the great majority goes counter to your ideal of discomfort. They prefer the surfaces, far less disquieting, whence their regrettable taste for symbols, which in a way, are an *explanatory surface*.

J.C. The depth breathes on the surface. The surfaces say, 'We breathe in the depths.' They always get away with it, and this is what causes our solitude.

A.F. To sum up, and to drive you to your last retrenchment, may I ask why you write and why you have your writings published? Why do you make plays, drawings and films?

J.C. It's probably the way in which my system eliminates. The function has created the organ. That is the only explanation I can think of that would account for my lack of modesty, my urge to spread out secrets in broad daylight for everyone to see.

A.F. What are you preparing now?

J.C. Nothing. Perhaps I've finished. Perhaps I have unwound my reel. Or perhaps it is only a halt. We'll have to wait and see. I could write plays, books and films. But I refuse. There are too many plays, books and films. Before I can sit down to work I must receive an order. That order comes from me, but from a 'me' whose aptitudes and mechanism I do not know. The

'I' who is speaking to you is but a vehicle for that other 'I'. As I have just been ill, perhaps the vehicle has incurred the temporary displeasure of that unknown 'I'. My role is to wait till it comes to a decision. I have been thinking of doing something that would be merely a new presentation of a French masterpiece, *Britannicus;* of presenting Racine in a new light, ridding him of the purring, the patina he has acquired in our schools. But as yet I am undecided. Sometimes a modest but very exacting job, that calls for a great deal of tiring effort, manages to excite our nocturnal factory and set it into motion. It may be have been that hope that made me think I would film *Britannicus*. Or perhaps I wanted to record Jean Marais's admirable Nero and to show him to everybody in his best role. I wonder. I seem to be less and less capable of analysing my own motives.

A.F. Are you waiting for inspiration? Do you believe in a force coming from the outside?

J.C. No. One should say 'expiration', not 'inspiration'. It is from our reserves, from our night that things come to us. Our work pre-exists within us. The problem is to discover it (*invenire*). We are merely its archaeologists.

NOTES AND POSTSCRIPTS

I am adding a few short notes. After the talk previously recorded, Jean Cocteau went on speaking. I feel that some of the things he said should be included in this book.

J.C. The strength of a film resides in its 'truthism', I mean, in its showing us things instead of telling them. Thus they are made to exist as facts, even if these facts rest upon the unreal or upon what the public is not accustomed to seeing.

Last year I saw at a film society the German film made by Leni Riefenstahl on the Olympic Games. The tragedy of that film was that it was acted by people who were dead, that a terrible foot had trodden on the ant heap. Moreover, the young audience was exceedingly nervous and a prey to political emotions. And yet after a few minutes the spectators were affected only

Le Baron Fantôme: scene. (Courtesy National Film Archive of the British Film Institute)

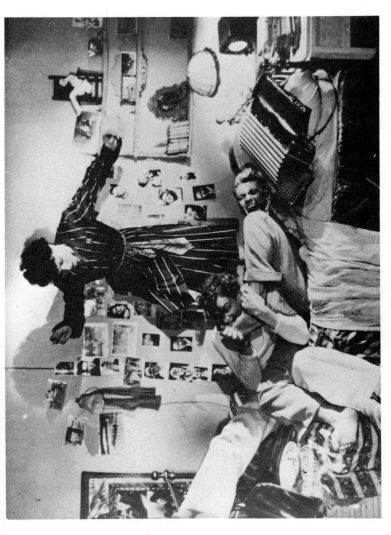

L'Eternel Retour: scene. (Courtesy National Film Archive of the British Film Institute)

L'Éternel Retour score. (Courtesy Ernest D. Burns of Cinemabilia)

L'Eternel Retour: scene. (Courtesy Ernest D. Burns of Cinemabilia)

L'Eternel Retour: scene. (Courtesy National Film Archive of the British Film Institute)

L'Eternel Retour: Jean Marais and Madeleine Sologne as
the lovers. (Courtesy Ernest D. Burns of Cinemabilia)

by the film's truth. It had become a newsreel. The audience was fascinated by the athletes and the games, and gave no more thought to the fact that the event they were watching was old, destroyed, dissolved. What one saw, one believed. The truth of moving images prevailed over everything else. It turned the film society audience into a stadium crowd. This is highly significant. It proves that there is nothing we cannot convey in a film, provided we succeed in investing it with a force of expression sufficient for changing our phantasms into undeniable facts.

But if our numbers weaken and our problem is posed without being solved, the public will see only a kind of superior legerdemain. It will notice the technique and the details of production, and will refuse to believe in the film itself. Production and technique should disappear for the sake of the truth that is ours, which must be able to convince the eye, the ear and the soul. Example: in the extraordinary film adapted by Melville from my *Les Enfants Terribles*, the slightest gesture of Nicole Stéphane took on the terrifying power of those of Electra. Thus emphasized by the acting, and by the Bach-Vivaldi music, the tragedy of little Elizabeth rose to such an intensity that it became embarrassing for the public and went beyond the compass of my book. What is seen is *seen.*

(Extract from a letter of April 20th, 1951):

The Festival at Cannes was superlatively organized and did credit to France. But it remains none the less true that a festival is always disturbing, and that the awards by referendum are the only acceptable ones. This race after rewards, run either by mediocre films or by films that are far beyond any awards (the Buñuel film, for instance) seems to me shocking and open to mistakes made all the more likely and dangerous by the tiredness of the jury. Too many festivals. Too many gala nights. Too many tournaments which have now lost whatever justification they might have had in the past, when the awards of the Biennale in Venice still had some sense. One leaves them overgorged with films, muddled, saddened, the soul full of stains that are slow to disappear. I would like to be free to re-make a film like *Le Sang d'un Poète*, but which would not be liked as *Le Sang d'un Poète* is liked *now*. A film that would disturb, as *Le Sang d'un Poète* disturbed in its day. There exists in France a tradition of anarchy (commonly called *avant-garde*) which we should respect just as any other tradition.

THE ISOU AFFAIR

(April, 1951)

(*A marginal note to the Cannes Festival*)

Isidore Isou invited us to *see* his film, which
he showed alongside the Festival. It was about
30,000 feet long. But he had finished only the
sound. He deemed his ideas sufficient for destroying the indigestible cinematograph. The
audience became restless, and he asked me to
speak to them. This is what I would have liked
to have said, but didn't say.

Isou claims, if I'm not mistaken, to carry out
a kind of vacuum-cleaning. But in that case the
vacuum should have a sucking force sufficient
for really cleaning the place out. When I show
Le Sang d'un Poète or *Orphée*, many people can't
see anything on the screen, but this is their fault
and not mine. Isou calls people imbeciles because they can't see what he doesn't show them.
But he could call them imbeciles only if they
didn't see what he does show them (be it even a
strip of celluloid that has been mangled on
purpose).

Moreover, in *Orphée* I gave my explanations
in advance. At the beginning of the film, the
revue *Nudisme* shows only a few blank pages.
'This is ridiculous,' says Orphée, and the
gentleman in the Café des Poètes replies: 'Less

ridiculous than if these pages were covered with a ridiculous text. Excess is never ridiculous.'

This is why what I really said to the audience was merely that an unusual atmosphere is always alive, and that Isou's strange performance deserves their welcome.

ESPERANTO OF A FILM

My film *Les Parents Terribles* is doing less well abroad than my other films. This is because the French language plays the leading part in it. The genius of the actors cannot overcome that difficulty. In *Orphée*, my ideas get through under the cover of the spectacle. This is what makes me hesitate about *Britannicus*. (*Hamlet* speaks a language of vast circulation.)

I will say it again: in order to reach a few we must be seen by all. Otherwise a book or a play would suffice.

The phenomenon we observe in all the arts, through which a brazen lie can convince people of a reality of a higher and deeper order, can be made to occur in a film only by an unusual use of people, gestures, words and places (a deliberate unusualness of costumes and settings would degenerate into a *masquerade*). It is only by a syntax of visual, common words placed in

136

a certain order that the lie of Art can be introduced into the cinematograph. I know only of *Caligari* where the lie was valid in spite of its operating in external forms.

Artistic creation is subject to the mechanism of all creation, which alters matter and appearance only by a different organisation of the same atoms.

LIST OF FILMS *

Le Sang d'un Poète

Director: Jean Cocteau.

Music: Georges Auric. *Art Director:* Jean Gabriel D'Eaubonne. *Director of Photography:* Périnal. *Accessories:* Maison Berthelin. The Flamant Orchestra under its Conductor, Edouard Flamant.
Cast: Lee Miller, Pauline Carton, Odette Talazac, Enrique Rivero, Jean Desbordes, Fernand Dichamps, Lucien Jager, Féral Benga, Barbette. *Editor:* Jean Wiedmer. *Stills:* Sacha Masour.

Le Baron Fantôme

Director and Scenarist: Serge de Poligny.

Dialogue: Jean Cocteau. *Assistant Director:* André Versein. *Production Manager:* Robert Florat. *Director of Photography:* Marc Fossard. *Assistant for shooting script:* Louis Chavance. *Costumes:* Christian Dior. *Camera Operator:* Roger Hubert. *Music (conducted by composer):* Louis Beydts. *Art Director:* Jacques Krauss. *Sound Engineer:* René Forget. *Montage:* Jean Feyte. *Continuity:* Chiffon Guillou. *Stills:* Aldo et Ancrenaz. *Stage manager:* Lucien Pinoteau.

* The chronological order of the films in this list is: *Le Sang d'un Poète, Le Baron Fantôme, L'Eternel Retour, La Belle et la Bête, Ruy Blas, Les Parents Terribles, L'Aigle à Deux Têtes* and *Orphée*. The list includes only the films up to the time this book was written in 1951.

138

Cast: André Lefaur, Odette Joyeux, Jany Holt, Alain Cuny, Gabrielle Dorziat, Alerme, Aimé Clariond (*Sociétaire de la Comédie-Française*), Claude Sainval, Marie Magali, Diener Peres, Marguerite Pierry.

Les Parents Terribles

Director: Jean Cocteau.

> *Designer:* Christian Bérard. *Music:* Georges Auric. *Director of Photography:* Michel Kelber. *Décor:* Guy de Gastyne. *Assistant Director and Editor:* Raymond Leboursier. *Camera Operator:* Tiquet. *Stills:* Corbeau. *Montage:* Jacqueline Sadoul. *Production:* Alexandre Nouchkine and Francis Cosne. *Cast:* Josette Day, Jean Marais, Yvonne de Bray, Marcel André, Gabrielle Dorziat.

L'Eternel Retour

Director: Jean Delannoy.

> *Script and Dialogue:* Jean Cocteau. *Music:* Georges Auric. *Director of Photography:* Roger Hubert. *Décor:* George Wakhevitch. *Production Manager:* Émile Darbon. *Production:* André Paulvé. *Stills:* Aldo.
> *Cast:* Madeleine Sologne, Jean Marais, Junie Astor, Jean Murat, Roland Toutain, Piéral, Jeanne Marken, Jean D'Yd, Alexandre Rignault, Yvonne de Bray.

Ruy Blas

From the play by Victor Hugo.

> *Script, adaptation and dialogue:* Jean Cocteau. *Director:* Pierre Billon. *Producers:* André Paulvé and Georges Legrand. *Assistant Director:* Michel Boisrond. *Production Manager:* René Jaspard. *Director of Photography:* Michel Kelber. *First Operator:* Louis

Stein. *Second Operator:* Roland Paillass. *Stage manager:* Lucien Pinoteau. *Music:* Georges Auric. *Décor:* Wakhevitch. *Costumes:* Escoffier. *Stills:* Raymond Voinquel.

Cast: Danielle Darrieux, Jean Marais, Gabrielle Dorziat, Marcel Herrand, Alexandre Rignault, Paul Amiot, Gilles Queant, Ionne Salinas, Jovanni Grasso, Charles Lemontier, Lurville, J. Berlioz, P. Magnier.

L'Aigle à Deux Têtes

Director: Jean Cocteau.

Music: Georges Auric. *Designer:* Christian Bérard. *Production:* Ariane Films, Sirius. *Technical Collaborator:* H. Bromberger. *Director of Photography:* Christian Matras. *Camera Operator:* Douarinou. *Décor:* Wakhevitch, Morin. *Accessories:* Pinoteau, Lemarchand. *Costumes:* Escoffier-Zay-Bataille. *Stills:* Raymond Voinquel.

Cast: Edwige Feuillère, Jean Marais, Jean Debucourt, Sylvia Monfort, Jacques Varennes, G. Queant, Abdallah, M. Mazyl, E. Stirling, Yvonne de Bray.

La Belle et la Bête

From the story by Madame LePrince de Beaumont.

Adaptation, dialogue and direction: Jean Cocteau. *Production:* André Paulvé. *Music:* Georges Auric. *Costumes:* Christian Bérard. *Décor:* Moulaert. *Assistant Director:* René Clément. *Production Manager:* Émile Darbon. *Director of Photography:* Alekan. *Stills:* Aldo.

Cast: Josette Day, Jean Marais, Mila Parely, Nane Germon, Michel Auclair, Marcel André.

140

Orphée

Written and directed by Jean Cocteau.

Presented by André Paulvé. *Music:* Georges Auric. *Director of Photography:* Nicolas Hayer. *Décor:* d'Eaubonne. *Costumes:* Escoffier. *Production Manager:* Émile Darbon. *Stills:* Nicolas Hayer.

Cast: Maria Casarès, Jean Marais, François Périer, Marie Dea, Henri Crémieux, Gréco, Edouard Dermit, Pierre Bertin, Jacques Varennes.

A CATALOGUE OF SELECTED DOVER BOOKS
IN ALL FIELDS OF INTEREST

A CATALOGUE OF SELECTED DOVER BOOKS
IN ALL FIELDS OF INTEREST

AMERICA'S OLD MASTERS, James T. Flexner. Four men emerged unexpectedly from provincial 18th century America to leadership in European art: Benjamin West, J. S. Copley, C. R. Peale, Gilbert Stuart. Brilliant coverage of lives and contributions. Revised, 1967 edition. 69 plates. 365pp. of text.

21806-6 Paperbound $3.00

FIRST FLOWERS OF OUR WILDERNESS: AMERICAN PAINTING, THE COLONIAL PERIOD, James T. Flexner. Painters, and regional painting traditions from earliest Colonial times up to the emergence of Copley, West and Peale Sr., Foster, Gustavus Hesselius, Feke, John Smibert and many anonymous painters in the primitive manner. Engaging presentation, with 162 illustrations. xxii + 368pp.

22180-6 Paperbound $3.50

THE LIGHT OF DISTANT SKIES: AMERICAN PAINTING, 1760-1835, James T. Flexner. The great generation of early American painters goes to Europe to learn and to teach: West, Copley, Gilbert Stuart and others. Allston, Trumbull, Morse; also contemporary American painters—primitives, derivatives, academics—who remained in America. 102 illustrations. xiii + 306pp.

22179-2 Paperbound $3.00

A HISTORY OF THE RISE AND PROGRESS OF THE ARTS OF DESIGN IN THE UNITED STATES, William Dunlap. Much the richest mine of information on early American painters, sculptors, architects, engravers, miniaturists, etc. The only source of information for scores of artists, the major primary source for many others. Unabridged reprint of rare original 1834 edition, with new introduction by James T. Flexner, and 394 new illustrations. Edited by Rita Weiss. 6⅝ x 9⅝.

21695-0, 21696-9, 21697-7 Three volumes, Paperbound $13.50

EPOCHS OF CHINESE AND JAPANESE ART, Ernest F. Fenollosa. From primitive Chinese art to the 20th century, thorough history, explanation of every important art period and form, including Japanese woodcuts; main stress on China and Japan, but Tibet, Korea also included. Still unexcelled for its detailed, rich coverage of cultural background, aesthetic elements, diffusion studies, particularly of the historical period. 2nd, 1913 edition. 242 illustrations. lii + 439pp. of text.

20364-6, 20365-4 Two volumes, Paperbound $6.00

THE GENTLE ART OF MAKING ENEMIES, James A. M. Whistler. Greatest wit of his day deflates Oscar Wilde, Ruskin, Swinburne; strikes back at inane critics, exhibitions, art journalism; aesthetics of impressionist revolution in most striking form. Highly readable classic by great painter. Reproduction of edition designed by Whistler. Introduction by Alfred Werner. xxxvi + 334pp.

21875-9 Paperbound $2.50

THE ARCHITECTURE OF COUNTRY HOUSES, Andrew J. Downing. Together with Vaux's *Villas and Cottages* this is the basic book for Hudson River Gothic architecture of the middle Victorian period. Full, sound discussions of general aspects of housing, architecture, style, decoration, furnishing, together with scores of detailed house plans, illustrations of specific buildings, accompanied by full text. Perhaps the most influential single American architectural book. 1850 edition. Introduction by J. Stewart Johnson. 321 figures, 34 architectural designs. xvi + 560pp.
22003-6 Paperbound $4.00

LOST EXAMPLES OF COLONIAL ARCHITECTURE, John Mead Howells. Full-page photographs of buildings that have disappeared or been so altered as to be denatured, including many designed by major early American architects. 245 plates. xvii + 248pp. 7⅞ x 10¾. 21143-6 Paperbound $3.50

DOMESTIC ARCHITECTURE OF THE AMERICAN COLONIES AND OF THE EARLY REPUBLIC, Fiske Kimball. Foremost architect and restorer of Williamsburg and Monticello covers nearly 200 homes between 1620-1825. Architectural details, construction, style features, special fixtures, floor plans, etc. Generally considered finest work in its area. 219 illustrations of houses, doorways, windows, capital mantels. xx + 314pp. 7⅞ x 10¾. 21743-4 Paperbound $4.00

EARLY AMERICAN ROOMS: 1650-1858, edited by Russell Hawes Kettell. Tour of 12 rooms, each representative of a different era in American history and each furnished, decorated, designed and occupied in the style of the era. 72 plans and elevations, 8-page color section, etc., show fabrics, wall papers, arrangements, etc. Full descriptive text. xvii + 200pp. of text. 8⅜ x 11¼. 21633-0 Paperbound $5.00

THE FITZWILLIAM VIRGINAL BOOK, edited by J. Fuller Maitland and W. B. Squire. Full modern printing of famous early 17th-century ms. volume of 300 works by Morley, Byrd, Bull, Gibbons, etc. For piano or other modern keyboard instrument; easy to read format. xxxvi + 938pp. 8⅜ x 11. 21068-5, 21069-3 Two volumes, Paperbound $10.00

KEYBOARD MUSIC, Johann Sebastian Bach. Bach Gesellschaft edition. A rich selection of Bach's masterpieces for the harpsichord: the six English Suites, six French Suites, the six Partitas (Clavierübung part I), the Goldberg Variations (Clavierübung part IV), the fifteen Two-Part Inventions and the fifteen Three-Part Sinfonias. Clearly reproduced on large sheets with ample margins; eminently playable. vi + 312pp. 8⅛ x 11. 22360-4 Paperbound $5.00

THE MUSIC OF BACH: AN INTRODUCTION, Charles Sanford Terry. A fine, nontechnical introduction to Bach's music, both instrumental and vocal. Covers organ music, chamber music, passion music, other types. Analyzes themes, developments, innovations. x + 114pp. 21075-8 Paperbound $1.25

BEETHOVEN AND HIS NINE SYMPHONIES, Sir George Grove. Noted British musicologist provides best history, analysis, commentary on symphonies. Very thorough, rigorously accurate; necessary to both advanced student and amateur music lover. 436 musical passages. vii + 407 pp. 20334-4 Paperbound $2.75

ALPHABETS AND ORNAMENTS, Ernst Lehner. Well-known pictorial source for decorative alphabets, script examples, cartouches, frames, decorative title pages, calligraphic initials, borders, similar material. 14th to 19th century, mostly European. Useful in almost any graphic arts designing, varied styles. 750 illustrations. 256pp. 7 x 10.   21905-4 Paperbound $4.00

PAINTING: A CREATIVE APPROACH, Norman Colquhoun. For the beginner simple guide provides an instructive approach to painting: major stumbling blocks for beginner; overcoming them, technical points; paints and pigments; oil painting; watercolor and other media and color. New section on "plastic" paints. Glossary. Formerly *Paint Your Own Pictures*. 221pp.   22000-1 Paperbound $1.75

THE ENJOYMENT AND USE OF COLOR, Walter Sargent. Explanation of the relations between colors themselves and between colors in nature and art, including hundreds of little-known facts about color values, intensities, effects of high and low illumination, complementary colors. Many practical hints for painters, references to great masters. 7 color plates, 29 illustrations. x + 274pp.
20944-X Paperbound $2.75

THE NOTEBOOKS OF LEONARDO DA VINCI, compiled and edited by Jean Paul Richter. 1566 extracts from original manuscripts reveal the full range of Leonardo's versatile genius: all his writings on painting, sculpture, architecture, anatomy, astronomy, geography, topography, physiology, mining, music, etc., in both Italian and English, with 186 plates of manuscript pages and more than 500 additional drawings. Includes studies for the Last Supper, the lost Sforza monument, and other works. Total of xlvii + 866pp. 7⅞ x 10¾.
22572-0, 22573-9 Two volumes, Paperbound $10.00

MONTGOMERY WARD CATALOGUE OF 1895. Tea gowns, yards of flannel and pillow-case lace, stereoscopes, books of gospel hymns, the New Improved Singer Sewing Machine, side saddles, milk skimmers, straight-edged razors, high-button shoes, spittoons, and on and on . . . listing some 25,000 items, practically all illustrated. Essential to the shoppers of the 1890's, it is our truest record of the spirit of the period. Unaltered reprint of Issue No. 57, Spring and Summer 1895. Introduction by Boris Emmet. Innumerable illustrations. xiii + 624pp. 8½ x 11⅝.
22377-9 Paperbound $6.95

THE CRYSTAL PALACE EXHIBITION ILLUSTRATED CATALOGUE (LONDON, 1851). One of the wonders of the modern world—the Crystal Palace Exhibition in which all the nations of the civilized world exhibited their achievements in the arts and sciences—presented in an equally important illustrated catalogue. More than 1700 items pictured with accompanying text—ceramics, textiles, cast-iron work, carpets, pianos, sleds, razors, wall-papers, billiard tables, beehives, silverware and hundreds of other artifacts—represent the focal point of Victorian culture in the Western World. Probably the largest collection of Victorian decorative art ever assembled— indispensable for antiquarians and designers. Unabridged republication of the Art-Journal Catalogue of the Great Exhibition of 1851, with all terminal essays. New introduction by John Gloag, F.S.A. xxxiv + 426pp. 9 x 12.
22503-8 Paperbound $4.50

POEMS OF ANNE BRADSTREET, edited with an introduction by Robert Hutchinson. A new selection of poems by America's first poet and perhaps the first significant woman poet in the English language. 48 poems display her development in works of considerable variety—love poems, domestic poems, religious meditations, formal elegies, "quaternions," etc. Notes, bibliography. viii + 222pp.

22160-1 Paperbound $2.00

THREE GOTHIC NOVELS: THE CASTLE OF OTRANTO BY HORACE WALPOLE; VATHEK BY WILLIAM BECKFORD; THE VAMPYRE BY JOHN POLIDORI, WITH FRAGMENT OF A NOVEL BY LORD BYRON, edited by E. F. Bleiler. The first Gothic novel, by Walpole; the finest Oriental tale in English, by Beckford; powerful Romantic supernatural story in versions by Polidori and Byron. All extremely important in history of literature; all still exciting, packed with supernatural thrills, ghosts, haunted castles, magic, etc. xl + 291pp.

21232-7 Paperbound $2.00

THE BEST TALES OF HOFFMANN, E. T. A. Hoffmann. 10 of Hoffmann's most important stories, in modern re-editings of standard translations: Nutcracker and the King of Mice, Signor Formica, Automata, The Sandman, Rath Krespel, The Golden Flowerpot, Master Martin the Cooper, The Mines of Falun, The King's Betrothed, A New Year's Eve Adventure. 7 illustrations by Hoffmann. Edited by E. F. Bleiler. xxxix + 419pp. 21793-0 Paperbound $2.50

GHOST AND HORROR STORIES OF AMBROSE BIERCE, Ambrose Bierce. 23 strikingly modern stories of the horrors latent in the human mind: The Eyes of the Panther, The Damned Thing, An Occurrence at Owl Creek Bridge, An Inhabitant of Carcosa, etc., plus the dream-essay, Visions of the Night. Edited by E. F. Bleiler. xxii + 199pp. 20767-6 Paperbound $1.50

BEST GHOST STORIES OF J. S. LEFANU, J. Sheridan LeFanu. Finest stories by Victorian master often considered greatest supernatural writer of all. Carmilla, Green Tea, The Haunted Baronet, The Familiar, and 12 others. Most never before available in the U. S. A. Edited by E. F. Bleiler. 8 illustrations from Victorian publications. xvii + 467pp. 20415-4 Paperbound $3.00

THE TIME STREAM, THE GREATEST ADVENTURE, AND THE PURPLE SAPPHIRE— THREE SCIENCE FICTION NOVELS, John Taine (Eric Temple Bell). Great American mathematician was also foremost science fiction novelist of the 1920's. *The Time Stream,* one of all-time classics, uses concepts of circular time; *The Greatest Adventure,* incredibly ancient biological experiments from Antarctica threaten to escape; The *Purple Sapphire,* superscience, lost races in Central Tibet, survivors of the Great Race. 4 illustrations by Frank R. Paul. v + 532pp.

21180-0 Paperbound $3.00

SEVEN SCIENCE FICTION NOVELS, H. G. Wells. The standard collection of the great novels. Complete, unabridged. *First Men in the Moon, Island of Dr. Moreau, War of the Worlds, Food of the Gods, Invisible Man, Time Machine, In the Days of the Comet.* Not only science fiction fans, but every educated person owes it to himself to read these novels. 1015pp. 20264-X Clothbound $5.00

THE PHILOSOPHY OF THE UPANISHADS, Paul Deussen. Clear, detailed statement of upanishadic system of thought, generally considered among best available. History of these works, full exposition of system emergent from them, parallel concepts in the West. Translated by A. S. Geden. xiv + 429pp.

21616-0 Paperbound $3.00

LANGUAGE, TRUTH AND LOGIC, Alfred J. Ayer. Famous, remarkably clear introduction to the Vienna and Cambridge schools of Logical Positivism; function of philosophy, elimination of metaphysical thought, nature of analysis, similar topics. "Wish I had written it myself," Bertrand Russell. 2nd, 1946 edition. 160pp.

20010-8 Paperbound $1.35

THE GUIDE FOR THE PERPLEXED, Moses Maimonides. Great classic of medieval Judaism, major attempt to reconcile revealed religion (Pentateuch, commentaries) and Aristotelian philosophy. Enormously important in all Western thought. Unabridged Friedländer translation. 50-page introduction. lix + 414pp.

(USO) 20351-4 Paperbound $2.50

OCCULT AND SUPERNATURAL PHENOMENA, D. H. Rawcliffe. Full, serious study of the most persistent delusions of mankind: crystal gazing, mediumistic trance, stigmata, lycanthropy, fire walking, dowsing, telepathy, ghosts, ESP, etc., and their relation to common forms of abnormal psychology. Formerly *Illusions and Delusions of the Supernatural and the Occult.* iii + 551pp. 20503-7 Paperbound $3.50

THE EGYPTIAN BOOK OF THE DEAD: THE PAPYRUS OF ANI, E. A. Wallis Budge. Full hieroglyphic text, interlinear transliteration of sounds, word for word translation, then smooth, connected translation; Theban recension. Basic work in Ancient Egyptian civilization; now even more significant than ever for historical importance, dilation of consciousness, etc. clvi + 377pp. 6½ x 9¼.

21866-X Paperbound $3.95

PSYCHOLOGY OF MUSIC, Carl E. Seashore. Basic, thorough survey of everything known about psychology of music up to 1940's; essential reading for psychologists, musicologists. Physical acoustics; auditory apparatus; relationship of physical sound to perceived sound; role of the mind in sorting, altering, suppressing, creating sound sensations; musical learning, testing for ability, absolute pitch, other topics. Records of Caruso, Menuhin analyzed. 88 figures. xix + 408pp.

21851-1 Paperbound $2.75

THE I CHING (THE BOOK OF CHANGES), translated by James Legge. Complete translated text plus appendices by Confucius, of perhaps the most penetrating divination book ever compiled. Indispensable to all study of early Oriental civilizations. 3 plates. xxiii + 448pp. 21062-6 Paperbound $3.00

THE UPANISHADS, translated by Max Müller. Twelve classical upanishads: Chandogya, Kena, Aitareya, Kaushitaki, Isa, Katha, Mundaka, Taittiriyaka, Brhadaranyaka, Svetasvatara, Prasna, Maitriyana. 160-page introduction, analysis by Prof. Müller. Total of 826pp. 20398-0, 20399-9 Two volumes, Paperbound $5.00

MATHEMATICAL PUZZLES FOR BEGINNERS AND ENTHUSIASTS, Geoffrey Mott-Smith. 189 puzzles from easy to difficult—involving arithmetic, logic, algebra, properties of digits, probability, etc.—for enjoyment and mental stimulus. Explanation of mathematical principles behind the puzzles. 135 illustrations. viii + 248pp.
20198-8 Paperbound $1.75

PAPER FOLDING FOR BEGINNERS, William D. Murray and Francis J. Rigney. Easiest book on the market, clearest instructions on making interesting, beautiful origami. Sail boats, cups, roosters, frogs that move legs, bonbon boxes, standing birds, etc. 40 projects; more than 275 diagrams and photographs. 94pp.
20713-7 Paperbound $1.00

TRICKS AND GAMES ON THE POOL TABLE, Fred Herrmann. 79 tricks and games—some solitaires, some for two or more players, some competitive games—to entertain you between formal games. Mystifying shots and throws, unusual caroms, tricks involving such props as cork, coins, a hat, etc. Formerly *Fun on the Pool Table*. 77 figures. 95pp.
21814-7 Paperbound $1.00

HAND SHADOWS TO BE THROWN UPON THE WALL: A SERIES OF NOVEL AND AMUSING FIGURES FORMED BY THE HAND, Henry Bursill. Delightful picturebook from great-grandfather's day shows how to make 18 different hand shadows: a bird that flies, duck that quacks, dog that wags his tail, camel, goose, deer, boy, turtle, etc. Only book of its sort. vi + 33pp. 6½ x 9¼.   21779-5 Paperbound $1.00

WHITTLING AND WOODCARVING, E. J. Tangerman. 18th printing of best book on market. "If you can cut a potato you can carve" toys and puzzles, chains, chessmen, caricatures, masks, frames, woodcut blocks, surface patterns, much more. Information on tools, woods, techniques. Also goes into serious wood sculpture from Middle Ages to present, East and West. 464 photos, figures. x + 293pp.
20965-2 Paperbound $2.00

HISTORY OF PHILOSOPHY, Julián Marias. Possibly the clearest, most easily followed, best planned, most useful one-volume history of philosophy on the market; neither skimpy nor overfull. Full details on system of every major philosopher and dozens of less important thinkers from pre-Socratics up to Existentialism and later. Strong on many European figures usually omitted. Has gone through dozens of editions in Europe. 1966 edition, translated by Stanley Appelbaum and Clarence Strowbridge. xviii + 505pp.
21739-6 Paperbound $3.00

YOGA: A SCIENTIFIC EVALUATION, Kovoor T. Behanan. Scientific but non-technical study of physiological results of yoga exercises; done under auspices of Yale U. Relations to Indian thought, to psychoanalysis, etc. 16 photos. xxiii + 270pp.
20505-3 Paperbound $2.50

Prices subject to change without notice.
Available at your book dealer or write for free catalogue to Dept. GI, Dover Publications, Inc., 180 Varick St., N. Y., N. Y. 10014. Dover publishes more than 150 books each year on science, elementary and advanced mathematics, biology, music, art, literary history, social sciences and other areas.

B&T 4 - 50 1